The Magic Bone

Michelle,
Thanks for reading our story.
Believe in miracles!

[signature]

The Magic Bone

THE STORY OF A BOY, A
MAGIC BONE, AND A TEAM
OF ANGELS. A MOTHER'S
ACCOUNT OF HER SON'S
MIRACULOUS RECOVERIES
FROM CANCER, A LIFE-
THREATENING INFECTION,
AND EPILEPSY

* * *

Jennifer Berreth

ISBN-13: 9780692950715
ISBN-10: 0692950710
Library of Congress Control Number: 2017915256
Jennifer Berreth, Lisbon, ND

Contents

CHAPTER 1

My Guardian Angel

* * *

I WOKE UP FROM A sound sleep. I opened my eyes and looked at the clock. It was just after one o'clock in the morning. I wondered for a split second why I had jolted awake. I couldn't remember my dreams. I had the funny feeling that someone was watching me. I glanced across the room to see a man standing in the corner. The instant I saw him, every hair on my body stood on end. I had a chill that covered me, and I held my breath.

Who is he? Why is he here? How did he get in here without me hearing anything? The house is one hundred years old. There is no way he got in here without someone waking up. The floor creaks with every step. Every door squeals upon opening, and the one in my room doesn't open without a good kick or swing of the hip. I glanced at the window. Did he come in through the window? I glanced at the door and the window. Both were closed tight. Should I scream for help? Maybe he has killed my entire family and is now waiting to take me.

All these thoughts raced through my head in a matter of seconds. When those few seconds of terror were over, I knew what he was. He was just that fuzzy image you see in the dark when you first wake up. Like the monster that comes out of the closet that isn't really a monster—just my eyes playing tricks on me. If I blink real hard, he'll change into something else and disappear. The only light in the room was from the streetlight outside and the alarm clock beside my bed. Blink, and he'll be gone. It seemed I had been staring at him for far too long. I blinked. He was still there. I blinked again. This time I held my eyes closed just a little longer. He was still there. It was not the fuzziness of waking up; he was still there. He didn't change shape and go away. He was exactly the same and was still standing there.

How long has this been going on? How long has it been since I've taken a breath? I breathed. I blinked some more. Harder, faster, hoping he just goes away. He was leaning on my vanity—his weight settled on his left leg. He slouched slightly in the shoulders. His arms were folded across his chest, and his chin rested in one hand. He's just in my imagination. He has to be. I closed my eyes again, this time for a long while, hoping this was all in my head, and he would be gone when I opened them again. I lay for what felt like forever. I opened my eyes again, and he was still there. Just watching me.

Does he know that I'm awake and can see him? What does he want? I wanted to scream. I wanted to get up and run. He would certainly catch me before I was able to beat my door open. If I screamed, no one would hear before he caught me. Maybe if I go back to sleep, he will just leave. What if I wake up and find he's hurt or killed my family? I closed my eyes again. "Please be gone; please be gone; please be gone," I chanted in my head. I opened my eyes. He was still there. This time he moved. He took his hand from his chin, folded it over his other arm, and shifted his weight from the left leg to the right. The floor creaked a little with his movement.

One more time I closed my eyes, hoping still that this was just my imagination, and I must have drifted off to sleep. When I opened my eyes again, it was 1:21 a.m., and he was gone. I heard nothing of him leaving. He was just gone.

When I opened my eyes again, the sun was shining through the window. There was no man standing in front of the vanity. The door and the window were still shut tight. Maybe I had been dreaming. I had an awful feeling that I might wake up to find my family had been murdered while I slept. I got out of bed and opened the door. I could hear chatting from the dining room below, and I felt relief that no one was dead or missing.

Then I was mad. Had my mom invited some drunk over to sleep it off on the couch? She was bartending at night while going to school and often let friends crash on the couch to prevent them from driving drunk or paying for a hotel. Someone was going to get an earful when I made it downstairs. Whoever she let in was a creep and had been in my room. The weirdo was probably sitting at the table having breakfast with them. I couldn't wait to get down there and find out who he was in the daylight and ask him what the hell he'd been doing in my bedroom. My parents would hear; he would be embarrassed and never come back to our house ever again.

I bounced down the stairs to find just my mom and dad drinking their coffee and reading the newspaper. I sat down at the table. I sat quietly for a minute and looked around the house. I didn't see anyone. Then I asked, "Did someone stay here last night?"

They both shot me a glance of confusion and looked at each other. I could almost read their thoughts. The look said silently, "Did you let someone in?" They looked back at me and replied with a quick, "No. Why?"

I said, "There was a man standing in my room last night, and I don't know who he was."

My mom sat with a puzzled look, like she didn't believe me. "Well, what was he doing?"

"Just standing there." I explained to them how I'd initially thought he was that sleepy fuzziness you get when you wake up at night, but he was there a long time. He'd even moved, I told them, and I could still see every detail of him.

My dad, looking somewhat panicked, stood up and asked us who'd forgotten to lock the damn door. He headed to the door to see if it was locked. He was checking the valuables—the safe, his guns, anything someone might want to steal. It didn't seem like anything was missing.

As my dad headed to the basement to check the cellar door and look for anything missing down there, I started describing the man to my mom. He was a very tall man. Tall enough that his head was over the mirror of the vanity by a foot or so. He must have been better than six feet by an inch or more. He was wearing a plaid flannel shirt. A dark color. Blue jeans and black shoes. His hair was thick, looked to be just black in the dark, and was combed to one side. He had shifted his weight a few times from one side to the other, almost like it bothered him to stand for too long.

My mom had a look on her face that I'd never seen before. It was a look of fear and joy at the same time. Like she had just watched a car run over her favorite dog, but then the dog jumped up and ran to her.

There was a little pause, and my dad emerged from the basement to say everything was fine and the door was locked down there too.

I said, "It must have been a ghost, then."

My dad laughed and said, "A ghost, huh?"

When the words left my mouth, I thought for a second and realized that my joke might be reality. "Yeah, a ghost." When I had been watching him watching me, I could see his back reflected in the mirror. I could see him, and I could see through him.

My mom's chin quivered, and a tear left one eye and then the other. "Oh my God," she said. "He was real."

My dad and I both stared at her in confusion.

"He was real?" I thought maybe this ghost was haunting her too, and she hadn't told us out of fear we would have her committed.

She said, "Well, Jennifer, you have a guardian angel."

"A what?"

"I think he was just stopping by to make sure you were okay."

"What?"

My mom proceeded to tell us a story, my dad and me, of her past experience with an angel who, at one time before my birth, promised her I would always be okay, and he would always be watching.

My mom was a young mom. Pregnant at fifteen, she'd been faced with some hard decisions. At the time of her pregnancy, my dad was not part of the big picture. My mom had decided to terminate her pregnancy. Not because she wanted to, but because it seemed like the only thing to do. My grandparents agreed with her decision, and my dad was not informed of it or even of my existence. An appointment was made. The end of my existence was scheduled to occur on March 10, 1980.

My mother had an uncle, Richard. Everyone knew him as Dick. I didn't know him. His passing was a tragic one and left my great-grandparents and many of his family and friends devastated. My mom said that Grandma and Grandpa were not the same people after he was gone. He'd suffered from a mental illness and taken his own life at the age of forty-three. My mom described this man to me and told stories of him in her childhood, stating that he was a wonderful man. One thing about him though was he put a fear of God into his nieces and nephews, and they all knew to not cross him. When he spoke, they listened! There was no telling more than once. She said he wasn't mean, but he just had that demeanor that kids feared. He was big and strong and had a great deep, booming voice. They didn't want Uncle Dick to holler, and when he did, there was silence, and they listened.

The day before the abortion coincidently was the same day Uncle Dick would have turned forty-five years old. My mom cried herself to sleep that night. She didn't want to do it, but what else could she do? In the middle of the night, she woke up.

That deep booming voice that she hadn't heard in so long shouted in her ear. "Don't do it!"

My mom sat straight up in bed. Dick wasn't there, but his voice was clear and so real that she could feel his breath in her ear.

"Don't do it!" he told her again. "Everything will be okay. I will be watching."

The next morning she woke up and told her parents she wasn't going to her appointment.

Grandpa's response was "Thank God."

My mother was very relieved; she'd thought the abortion was what both he and my grandma wanted her to do.

She never told anyone what she heard until this morning after he stood in my room watching me sleep.

I was feeling very relieved at this moment that I was alive and well. My life was pretty great up to this point, and I was glad my mother didn't go through with her abortion. I was an only child for the first seven years of my life and the only grandchild for a long while. I was everyone's first baby. I had an overabundance of people to spoil me. I always had fun places to go and fun things to do, but my favorite place was with Grandma Agnes. This grandma was Dick's mom, and her sadness over losing her only son lessened greatly when I came along.

I spent hours and days with Grandma Agnes and Grandpa Frank. Mowing, gardening, exploring the town with Grandpa. Grandma had me sitting on her lap learning to crochet and do needlepoint; I could whip up a plastic canvas Kleenex box cover in minutes. I could decorate an entire Christmas tree with my canvas creations in a matter of hours, and I did. I learned to love coffee before I could walk and learned it tasted better when shared with friends. As my mom continued to tell me stories of Uncle Dick, I learned it was at Grandma's house that I had my first encounter with him, and I had many encounters—I was just too little to remember.

When I was a toddler, during the many hours I spent with Grandma, I had a "friend." This imaginary friend I would play with most often at Grandma's house. I played with my friend quite a bit, because Grandma's house was where I was most of the time. That's where I always wanted to be.

There were certain things I was allowed to do at Grandma's house that other grandkids before me were never allowed to do, and climbing and playing on the steps was one. Grandma discouraged me from going up there and would often make me come down, but I would go right back up. I didn't get in too much trouble. I just got a talk about how playing up there was dangerous and I could fall down the stairs. They were very steep and narrow. I would inform Grandma that I was playing with my friend and that he wasn't going to let me fall.

I was small, and kids have imaginary friends all the time, so Grandma didn't argue, but she knew my friend wasn't real and I would eventually fall and break some part of my body. One day Grandma was fed up with me not listening and always going up the stairs, and we argued. She yelled at me that I had to get down from there this minute!

I insisted that I was never going to fall down the stairs because my friend wasn't going to let me.

She snapped back at me, saying there was no one up there with me and to stop this nonsense and get back downstairs.

I told her, "There is someone up here with me, and he's not going to let me fall."

"Who is your friend, and where is he? I don't see him."

We kept arguing, and I insisted that she did know my friend and I didn't know why she couldn't see him—he was right there with me!

I finally came down the stairs and escorted her to the group of photos hanging in the hallway. "This is my friend, right here!" I was pointing at Dick's high-school graduation photo hanging on the wall. We didn't argue about playing on the steps anymore.

I didn't see Dick again after that night I found him watching me sleep. I did have a very vivid dream about him once and woke up to his hands covering me with a blanket. In the dream, I was lost. It seemed like I was in a basement somewhere. I kept looking for a way out and was walking and walking. I was so cold and tired. Every time I found a door, I would open it to find a solid brick wall behind it. Finally, a door appeared in front of me, and I knew this one was the way out. I put my hand on the doorknob and glanced behind me. I felt as if someone was watching me, and there he was. Leaning on what looked like a big rusty pipe. I gave him a look, and it was as if he was reading my mind. "What do I do?" was my thought, and with a smile and a nod of his head, he was telling me, "Go ahead. You'll be okay."

Just like that the dream ended. I was lying in my bed. I felt this heaviness over my body and such an ice-cold chill. It was hard to breathe, and I was so cold. I sat up partway to reach for my blanket and try to catch my breath. As I opened my eyes and sat up to reach, I froze. Two hands were already on my blanket. They seemed to belong to no one. They covered me up as I moved backward. Back toward my bed. All the cold was suddenly gone, and I could breathe again. I felt warm and very safe despite what I'd just seen. I was going to be okay. Whatever that dream was about or whatever was coming my way, I was going to be okay.

A few short months after that dream, I learned I was pregnant. I was only seventeen years old. I had big plans for my life. I wanted to join the military, go to college, travel the world, and have a career in some aspect of music before I had any kids. And now, a baby. I was having a baby. I knew we would be okay. No matter what, we would be okay.

CHAPTER 2

Pregnant at Seventeen

* * *

GETTING PREGNANT AT SEVENTEEN WASN'T exactly part of
my big plans for life. It was something very unexpected,
and I didn't have much time to plan for anything. I learned
of my pregnancy on September 20, 1998, and to my surprise, I also learned the very same day that I was having a
boy. My due date was set for January 29, 1999.

How does a girl go a whole twenty-two weeks into
a pregnancy and not know she's pregnant? That's what I
wonder to myself all the time. I suspected I was pregnant
early in the summer. Sometime in the middle of June.
Instead of taking a home pregnancy test, I went straight
to the gynecologist with my pregnancy concerns. He
questioned my birth-control use. Was I taking it regularly
and at roughly the same time every day? Yes and yes. He
somewhat laughed off my concerns and told me girls my
age were rarely regular. He wrote up a prescription for a
different kind of birth-control pill and sent me on my way.
I didn't question him; he was the doctor, and I figured he
knew better than me.

The new birth control he sent me home with was one to start the Sunday after your menstrual period. I was never really sure when that was all summer, so I never started the pill.

I had some common pregnancy symptoms, but I didn't know at the time they were symptoms of being pregnant. Little things that could easily be blamed on other stuff. I was seventeen, with a very busy schedule. I was in every extracurricular activity possible in the summer, had an active social life, and worked three jobs. To say I was exhausted was an understatement. I was tired all day, every day, through the entire summer. I blamed it on my hectic schedule. If I ever was sitting, I was sleeping. Whether that was straight up on a chair, the couch, or outside in the grass. Since I rarely made it to my bed to sleep—because I would fall asleep wherever I sat—I often missed out on brushing my teeth before bed. When my gums started bleeding every day, I just blamed it on not brushing and flossing as well and often as I should be. On the days that I did make it to my bed, whenever I was lying flat, I would wake up with the worst charley horses. They were so bad I would almost cry. I blamed those on dehydration. I thought for sure dance camp did me in, and these cramps were never going away. Eight solid hours of sweating for two weeks in one-hundred-degree heat was surely the cause. I upped my consumption of bananas and Gatorade and went about my life.

I wasn't aware of any of these things being a normal part of pregnancy until I learned I was pregnant. I didn't have the common symptoms like morning sickness, weight gain, and weird food cravings. I actually lost weight over the summer. It wasn't until September that I suspected again that I might be pregnant. I didn't think I was pregnant through the whole summer. I guessed I got that way sometime later in the summer from not taking my birth-control pills and other methods being faulty.

One night in September, after a football game, I went to a party. Fully loaded with a liter of peach schnapps and a gallon of orange juice, I was ready to whoop it up. I didn't drink all summer long because I was so busy and always tired, so this was the night. Being from a small town in North Dakota, I was somewhat of a seasoned drinker at this point in my life. I could almost drink my dad under the table by the time I was fifteen. Not something to be proud of, but that's just how it was around there. Nothing to do but drink...and sometimes get pregnant. Even though I drank often, I was usually responsible about it—finding a designated driver and having some bail money stashed away in case I got caught. I rode to the party with friends, and my uncle was going to drive us home.

Once we pulled into the party, I mixed my first drink on the tailgate of the pickup. I didn't get halfway through my first glass before the nausea hit me like a ton of bricks. My stomach was making noises like I'd never heard, and I felt like I'd never felt before. I was hot and sweaty, and by this point in the year, the nighttime air was pretty chilly. I shed my hoodie, but nothing helped.

I told my uncle that I needed to get out of there. "Someone needs to take me home or to the farm; I need a toilet real fast so I don't shit my pants at this party." He and some of my friends laughed hysterically at me. No joke, though; I was dead serious. Something gross was about to happen. I wasn't sure what end it was going to come from, but I didn't want to be standing around at a party if it was the bottom end, and that's what it was feeling like.

When they finished laughing at me and realized how sick I actually looked, they headed behind me to the pickup. I'm somewhat of a country girl, and I'm not afraid to "prairie squat," but I wasn't country enough to poop on the prairie when a perfectly good toilet was only five miles away. I only made it to the top of the hill where the pickup was parked before everything came out. Thank goodness it wasn't coming from the end I expected it to.

More laughter erupted from the three standing behind me. One of them came to my rescue and grabbed hold of my long hair while I heaved unexpectedly and abruptly. The other two pointed, laughed, and said, "I thought you had to poop." My middle fingers were waving in the air in their direction as they continued to laugh. Things came out of me that I swear were inside me since first grade. It was like I was exorcising a demon. It just didn't quit.

When it was finally over, I opted not to take another drink. I stayed at the party but replaced my schnapps with a gallon of water. I felt like I hadn't drunk anything for days. I came to the realization then that I was probably pregnant.

The very next day I got myself a home pregnancy test instead of a doctor's appointment. I sent a friend to pick one up in the nearest Walmart because I was not going to be seen grabbing one off the shelf in the local drugstore. The whole town would have me pregnant in under ten minutes, even if I wasn't. I argued with myself in my head, saying it was just bad orange juice. It was a stomach bug. I was just too exhausted to be out so late.

Then I had the what-if-I-am-pregnant talks in my head. Do I keep it? I can't have an abortion. I knew I couldn't live with myself if I did that. Should I give it up for adoption? What if the people who take it are mean? I was calling it an *it*, so "it" wasn't really real to me yet. Just a small possibility. Do I have enough money to raise it? What would I name it? Can I really do this?

As soon as school let out on Monday afternoon, I went to the nearest bathroom that wasn't my own and peed on the stick. It was positive. My guts were turning, and I felt dizzy. Maybe it's wrong. It was a two-for-one pack so I peed on the next stick. Positive again. I didn't really know what to do, who to tell, or where to go. I just sat there with my little pink stick with the positive result and stared for what felt like hours. I needed to find a doctor before I did anything. I most certainly wasn't going back to the one who laughed at me when I thought I was pregnant a few months ago. Had I been pregnant this whole time? I couldn't have been. I should have known it by now. I should have been sick and had tight pants by now. The sickness came, but only a couple of days ago.

I told one family member of my positive test in hopes that she could point me in the direction of a good doctor. She was also pregnant, so I went to her for advice. I called the clinic right away the next morning. I explained my situation of having suspected I was pregnant a few months ago, not taking a home test, and not starting my new birth control. They usually didn't see pregnant patients until after eight weeks, but I had absolutely no idea how long this had been going on so they decided I should be seen right away. I was scheduled for that Wednesday afternoon. I couldn't get anything late enough to not skip out of school for a couple of hours.

Now I had to cook up some lie to tell my parents to excuse me from school early. I didn't want to tell them I thought I might be pregnant and needed to see a doctor right away. Because what if I wasn't? The likelihood of that home test being wrong twice was pretty unlikely, but I was going to hold on to some shred of hope.

I had one whole day to come up with some good excuse to get out of school. I had no idea what to say, but I had to think of something fast. It was all I could think about the entire eight hours I sat in school, but nothing came to me. That night on the local television channel, there was a commercial for the movie *Titanic* being released on VHS and DVD. Perfect! It wasn't a good excuse to skip school, but my parents were lenient and knew how much I loved that movie, plus I had good grades, so I didn't figure they'd say no. "Can I leave school early tomorrow?" I asked my dad.

"What the hell for?"

"The *Titanic* is coming out at three o'clock, and I need to get it before it sells out."

I got a that's-so-dumb look from him, but he said okay and wrote a note to excuse me from school at two o'clock.

I arrived at the clinic just before three o'clock a nervous wreck. I was both nervous and scared. I brought my checkbook to pay for the appointment because I didn't want insurance to be billed or what was left after insurance to land in my dad's mailbox.

The appointment was busy. So many questions, so much blood work. And then the result. I was definitely pregnant, but for how long was yet to be determined. Based on the questions the doctor asked and the last time I had a normal period, he wanted to do an ultrasound right away. His best guess from the ultrasound was I was right around twenty-one to twenty-two weeks.

He asked me, "Do you want to know the sex?"

"Holy, what? Are you kidding me?" was my thought. "I guess so."

"It's a boy!"

My jaw was on the floor. I really was pregnant the first time I went to a doctor and was laughed right out the door with a packet of birth-control pills. I was fuming mad.

The due date for my baby boy was set: January 29, 1999. Everything looked good and normal.

Now what? What do I do now? I didn't even have much time to think about it. Twenty-two weeks? This baby was already half-done, and I didn't even know. It was only a matter of time before I would start to get very thick in the middle and not be able to hide this from anyone. I wanted to. Maybe I could run away somewhere and never tell anyone. I had the funds to do it. How do I tell everyone? What do I say? How can I do this? Can I really do this? I thought about adoption again and thought about it over and over. Could I really do that? I would likely drive myself completely insane wondering about him all the time. I decided that really wasn't the best thing. What if he ended up in the hands of child molesters or some weird people like that? The thought of it made me cringe.

I spent the next week crunching numbers, figuring out how much day care and rent cost. I calculated college tuition and how big of a paycheck I could collect while attending college. Was it even possible to work full time with a baby and college? Could I make it working part time? Could I get assistance? Would my family help me, or would they be too mad? So many questions, so little time. After all my crunching, I figured that I could still go to college, work part time, and make it on my own with no help from anyone. Now all I had left to figure out was how to tell everyone and hope like hell my parents didn't throw me out of the house.

The week after my clinic visit and the week I had it all figured out was the same week I busted out of my size-seven jeans and felt the first kick. The first kick I felt was on September 27 around two o'clock in the afternoon. He didn't start with any small movements. He started big. A whole entire acrobatic routine right off the bat while I was sitting quietly in English class. It was the strangest feeling I've ever had. It tickled at first and startled me so much that I let out a loud squeal and started giggling because of the sound I made. It wasn't unusual for me to burst out laughing at odd times at absolutely nothing, so no one even questioned my behavior. Wearing sweatpants every day was unusual for me so I had to start thinking about telling people before they questioned my new fashion change.

I started with my grandma. I thought she'd be the easiest to tell since she had gone through three of her kids being pregnant as teens. She was easy. One aunt already knew, plus a few close friends. The two people I was most scared to tell were my mom and my great-grandma Agnes. I decided to tell my mom in a letter. Let her know I was pregnant and show her my plan of how it was going to work. Tell her I was still going to college and how. I would leave it in her car on my way to school. The cowardly thing to do. Drop it and run. I was safe that way for a whole eight hours. I was safe from murder or torture and homelessness or whatever was coming to me after eight hours. I had eight hours to think about where I was going to live if I no longer had a home at 3:20 p.m.

I tossed the letter on the front seat of her car on my way out the next morning. I wasn't quick enough. She caught me!

"What was that?"

"Umm, I wrote you a letter. Just read it later; I'm going to be late." And I tried to walk away.

"Wait a minute. What does it say?"

"Just read it." My voice started to crack as I started to cry. Damn you, hormones!

"Jennifer, what does it say? You're not pregnant, are you?"

"Yes, I am. Just read the letter; I have to get to school." I walked away in tears and left my mom just standing there in the driveway. The very last thing she ever wanted me to do I just did.

The whole day in school was torture. Because my mom now knew, I told a few more people in school. Friends and a couple of teachers. It wasn't going to be long before I couldn't participate in some of my extracurricular activities such as dancing and cheerleading. Once my belly got big enough, those things were going to be difficult. I didn't have to quit music, and I was happy about that. That was the stuff I was good at. By the end of that week, everyone who needed to know knew I was pregnant, except my two old grandmas. I was scared to death to tell them, and so was everyone else. Mostly Great-Grandma Agnes.

Finally, in the middle of the next week, I dragged myself kicking and screaming to Grandma's house. I brought a lot of family with me for backup. We gathered in the hallway to discuss our game plan and argue over who was going to tell her. I didn't want to, so I unsuccessfully tried to convince everyone else to do it for me.

One of Grandma's closest friends, Pearl, was also there, and she came around the corner to give me a firm talking-to. No one breathed the whole time she spoke, which didn't take long because she could talk sixty miles a minute. "Jesus Christ, I don't know what the hell's the matter with all of you. Someone has to tell her already. Just look at how damn fat you're getting, and you can't just not come over here anymore 'cause then she's going to wonder where the hell you're at and what's going on." And just like that, because we all were "too chickenshit," she turned the corner on her fancy shoes, sat down at the table, and blurted out, "Jen's having a baby in January, and there's no sense in getting pissed about it. It is what it is."

As we all stood there with our mouths wide open, waiting for the fury of "Hurricane Agnes," she smiled and said, "Why didn't you tell me?"

Our mouths were still wide open, and we were shocked.

"Well, you didn't think I'd love you any less because you're having a baby, did you?"

Some colorful four-letter words were mumbled by those who'd gone before me and were standing behind me for backup.

Pearl erupted in laughter and slapped her knee. "You didn't think Jennifer could do any wrong, did you?" And she laughed some more, while everyone else scowled in disbelief.

"Come over here, and sit on your old grandma's lap," Grandma Agnes said.

More looks of anger and four-letter words came from my backup crew, which consisted of my grandma, mom, and aunt. I had a cocky look on my face because they were the ones who had convinced me that this would be so horrible, and it wasn't so bad.

Grandma Agnes quickly got to work making blankets, hats, and booties. It was her first great-great-grandchild, and she was more excited than anyone.

We had stopped at the other great-grandma's house prior to going to Agnes's. We weren't as scared of her reaction, but it was still hard to tell her.

She shook her head and said, "You'll be all right; this will all work out."

We just sat in silence for a minute.

"You're not going to get married, are you?"

"I have no immediate plans to."

"Good; you shouldn't." A little surprising coming from someone who was just shy of ninety years old and grew up in a time when, if you were pregnant, you married, whether you wanted to or not. "Just because you test-drive a car doesn't mean you have to buy it. You can test-drive a lot of cars before you invest in one that you really want. And that's okay. You understand this old lady?"

"Yes, I do."

The hardest part of my pregnancy—telling my old grandmas—was over. The rest of my pregnancy was smooth sailing. A few kicks here and there. I never missed a day of school because of it. I remained active in everything I could and planned for the arrival of my baby boy. I decided his name was Ethan before I even knew for sure I was pregnant. Toward the end of the pregnancy, I developed preeclampsia. My blood pressure was elevated, and I blew up like a balloon. I gained a total of twenty-five pounds, and most of those pounds came during the last week. Ethan was due on January 29, and the time went so fast.

CHAPTER 3

Ethan's Arrival

* * *

ETHAN ARRIVED ON JANUARY 19, 1999, ten days ahead of schedule. My blood pressure was steadily on the rise, and I was retaining water, so it was decided that I would be induced on the morning of January 19 to prevent further complications. The pregnancy was a breeze, and the labor was easy, but the delivery was a small disaster.

I arrived at the hospital at seven o'clock that morning. I was taken into a small private hospital room by the nurse who checked me in. I was given instructions to remove all my clothes and put on a lovely floral print, less-than-comfortable hospital gown. Once I was finished, she would return to check my cervix and call the doctor to see how he would like to proceed, depending on the progress of my labor. The previous week, I was already dilated to five, with no other signs of labor than an occasional small contraction. The contractions I had were many, many hours apart and not painful at all. When the nurse returned, she checked me over and decided I was still at five. The doctor was on his way and would get things moving along.

The doctor came in, made a little small talk, and told me what he was going to do and what I could expect. I nodded in agreement, having no idea what was about to really happen. He explained that he would break my water and encouraged me to get up and do a lot of walking when he was finished as that would help move things along. He pointed in the direction of some very cozy-looking adult diapers in the corner near the sink and advised that I not go without one of those while I was moving about outside of my bed. He joked that no one wanted to walk around behind me cleaning up puddles because the staff was already busy enough. He pulled out a very long, sharp-looking object that seemed like a giant crochet hook.

"You're putting that where?"

"This is what we use to rupture the membranes." The words *rupture* and *membranes* made my skin crawl. He inserted the large hook. There was a weird snapping sound. It felt like popping a water balloon that was lodged up inside my body, and the noises it made matched the feeling. Just a weird squeaky snap.

There was no pain, but a huge release of pressure, and what felt like fifty pounds of fluid came gushing out of me. "Wow! That felt great," I said out loud.

The doctor raised his eyebrows as he looked at me and laughed. He said he doesn't hear that very often, and he patted my knee as he stood up and told me I probably wasn't going to be feeling that great the next time he popped in to check on me, which would be in a couple of hours. Again, he encouraged me to get up and walk, so that's what I did.

As soon as he left, I slid on my ever-so-comfortable diaper, grabbed my IV pole, and headed out the door. I got bored real fast looking at the same scenery, and I didn't feel any different so I headed back to my room to see what was on the TV.

The company started flooding in around nine. By the time lunchtime came around, I had a whole room full of aunts, uncles, cousins, friends, and grandparents there to meet the new baby boy.

Once I was back in my bed, the nurse came in, cleared everyone out, and inspected my cervix once again. Still at five. She put a big elastic belt over my belly with a monitor for the baby's heartbeat and to measure the intensity of my contractions. There were contractions, but they seemed to be small and not real close together yet. She informed me that the doctor would be up to make rounds shortly and they might bring some drugs on board to help move things along.

The doctor stopped in and repeated what the nurse had just told me. "Make a couple of more laps around the floor, and I'll be back after lunch. If there is no more progress, we'll start some Pitocin in your IV." I just nodded and agreed once again, having no idea what that was. He explained it was a hormone that would make the labor progress a little faster.

So I got up and made a few more laps. Nothing happened. I got back into bed and all restrapped with my monitors. I watched TV and visited with everyone who was just hanging around waiting.

Around one o'clock the nurse came in to check my progress again. I was beginning to feel very violated. I don't think I exposed my body parts this much to get the baby in there, and it seemed excessive to get him out. The doctor didn't come back since the last visit a couple of hours ago, but he did leave orders to start the Pitocin, so that's what the nurse was going to do.

Everyone who was there to visit decided they were going to be there for the rest of the day waiting on the baby, so they all left to grab some lunch. Everyone except my brother. He wasn't going to miss anything, so he sat right by my bed flipping through TV channels as I lay there waiting for something exciting to happen.

It was just around one thirty when the nurse put the Pitocin in my IV, and it wasn't long after that I started to feel very uncomfortable. There was a lot of pressure in places that I didn't want there to be pressure and a very uncomfortable burning in the area of both of my ovaries. Not real painful, just slightly uncomfortable. I called the nurse. "I'm feeling a lot of pressure."

She checked the contraction monitor and suggested a bedpan.

Yuk! No! So up to the bathroom I went. "I don't think the bathroom is the answer. I think maybe this baby boy is ready to exit."

"Oh no, honey, you're hardly having any contractions," she told me as she's studied the monitor.

So I went back to bed. The pressure got much worse in the next few minutes, and I started to sweat profusely. Again, I called the nurse. "Are you sure this baby isn't ready to come out?"

She looked again at the monitor. "Oh no, honey, this could go on for hours; you're not ready yet."

"Okay." I believed these people were the experts on birthing children, so I just sat there in my misery for another ten minutes and waited. Then I had to push. There was no getting around it. My body was just pushing. I was making funny grunting noises that I couldn't control.

My brother, who was still sitting next to me, had the weirdest look on his face and said, "I'm calling that nurse back here."

Good idea. I didn't want to bother her again because I assumed she knew better than me and, by guessing her age, she had assisted in delivering babies for far longer than I had been alive.

She walked in, and I immediately told her, "I have to push. I'm pushing, and I can't control it."

She looked at the monitor again and again said, "Oh no, honey…"

The words no sooner left her mouth than my entire upper body heaved forward off the bed and noise came with my motions that I couldn't make on a normal day if I tried.

The nurse just stared at me for a moment and watched me with a look of disbelief and guilt on her face; the look on my brother's face was that of terror, like he was watching an exorcism or a real-life monster. After my body relaxed, the nurse said nervously, "Let's check you again and see how things are coming along." She put on some gloves, and I could feel the pushing sensation coming back almost instantly after I relaxed. She didn't even get her fingers anywhere near where they were going, and she had a very worried look on her face. "Okay, honey, try not to push for a minute; I have to get the doctor."

She didn't even get all the way out the door, and I was pushing again. "Try not to push" was an impossible request.

When she returned, she brought a whole team of new people in with her and a bunch of equipment. Some of them came to the end of my bed; a couple of others just stood in the front of the room. They were all scrambling to put on gloves and gowns and plug things in. I could tell by the looks they gave me and the feeling I had when the nurse last checked things that there was a baby right down there between my legs, just hanging out. He was just hanging out waiting for me to finish pushing him out or someone to grab him and pull him out, and no one in the room seemed to know exactly what to do. Help maybe, was what I was thinking.

The family all started flooding back into the room, which was now suddenly a delivery room.

"The baby is ready; we're just waiting for the doctor," the nervous nurse told everyone as they walked through the door.

The doctor walked in, raised his eyebrows, and said, "Oh my, looks like we're having a baby right here." He put on one glove and instantly put that one hand between my legs to start tugging at things and told me to give a good push. While he was tugging with one hand, he was holding his other hand straight up in the air while the nurse was attempting to put a glove on his other hand. Two more pushes, and there was a tiny baby boy, right there on the bottom of my bed.

He was a very unfortunate-looking, tiny baby boy. His head was misshapen. He was a complete cone head, and he had big red splotches all over his body. Other than his funny look from being trapped in the birth canal for far too long, he was perfect. Ten fingers, ten toes, a squeaky but powerful cry, and the biggest blue eyes ever. We remained in the hospital for a couple of short days, and then we went home.

Life as a Teen Mom

* * *

THE LIFE OF A TEEN mom really wasn't as horrible as people made it sound. I was expecting to have a constant struggle in my day-to-day life, and it was nothing like that. Ethan was a very good baby, and that probably helped. He slept a solid six hours every night within the first two weeks of his life and rarely ever cried. The only time I ever heard a sound out of him was when he was hungry or his diaper was wet. I don't even know if I'd call it a real cry; it was more of a "hey, I'm uncomfortable" squeak. I was able to return to school in just a couple of weeks, and I ducked in and out several times a day to check up on him. Fortunately we were able to get a spot in a day care just a couple of steps outside the back door of my high school. I carried on with all my extracurricular activities that I hadn't given up during the pregnancy and was even able to go back to work for a few hours here and there. Ethan had an abundance of grandmas, great-grandmas, and even great-great-grandmas who were more than happy to steal him away from me for a few hours during the week so I could carry on my normal life. In addition to grandmas, he also had aunts, uncles, cousins, and my friends who couldn't get enough of him. Everything carried on as normal; I now just had a quiet little sidekick whom I was responsible for.

I graduated from high school on May 27, 1999, and Ethan and I had plans to move to Bismarck so I could attend college. I found him a great day care and enrolled in classes for that fall. Plans changed a little over the summer, and I decided I would be able to work more and save more money if I remained in my hometown for the first year of college. We were able to rent a small two-bedroom house just across the street from both of his grandparents, and that's where we stayed for the next year.

Things went along very smoothly for Ethan's first year. I went to school for a few hours a day, and he went to the new day care. In the summer of 2001, we finally ventured to the big city. I found a two-bedroom apartment for about the same price I was paying on my house. I was able to find not one, but two, jobs before the move, and I transferred to the local community college from the university, with a different major and a much smaller price tag. I decided that a career as a music teacher wasn't going to be my thing, so I took up nursing. I was still able to get a music scholarship by playing in the band. We had to switch day care because the one we had wasn't able to hold a spot for us over the summer months. We quickly settled into an everyday routine once school started, and Ethan was the happiest kid ever. We were both happy and content. Life was good.

Our schedule didn't vary much from week to week. Every day started around eight o'clock. Ethan went to day care on school days—Monday, Wednesday, and Friday—and his dad picked him up at four. On nonschool days he would come to the gym with me and spend the rest of the day with me and go with his dad at five o'clock. Every other weekend we would head home on Sunday to spend the afternoon with family. The best part of Ethan's Sunday trips home was going to see Grandma Elsa. Elsa was his favorite, and Ethan was hers.

CHAPTER 5

Losing Grandma Elsa

* * *

GRANDMA LEFT US EARLY IN the morning on March 30, 2001, at the young age of ninety-two. Her relationship with Ethan was a special one.

We had our regular routine of visits to Grandma every other Sunday, and when we left her, he was already asking every time when we could go back, once he was able to talk. He couldn't wait to see her and was so excited every time we were there. It was almost like they were soul mates. They both beamed with happiness when they saw each other, and you couldn't wipe the smiles from their faces if you tried. Every time we were there to visit, they would sit in the chair, and Grandma would bounce him on her knee and tickle him with her knuckles; he would laugh until he couldn't breathe, and Grandma would laugh at his laughter. They would dance to the best of Grandma's ability on her bad knees. Ethan would run away from her, and she would yell, "Get over here, and sit with this old grandma." Ethan would run away and laugh, and she would say it over again in a game of catch me if you can. In my whole life, I had not seen Grandma as jolly as she was when Ethan was around.

Once Ethan was born, Grandma did extra things like stick extra money in my Christmas cards. I would get "thinking of you" cards in the mail with a five-dollar bill taped inside and signed with "very, very much love."

The week that Grandma passed was the same week Ethan, my very well-behaved toddler, had his first ever temper tantrum. It was a Wednesday night, and he did it at the most inconvenient time. While my arms were fully loaded with groceries and with three flights of stairs in front of me, he asked to go see Grandma Elsa.

I said, "No, we can't until Sunday."

That was not a sufficient answer, so he yelled, "I want to see Grandma Elsa right now!"

I was very surprised at his behavior, but at his age, I should have expected him to behave like this, and he never did. So I thought, "Here start the terrible twos a little behind schedule." He started insisting when we got out of the car. I lifted him from his car seat and grabbed the groceries, and we argued about it all the way to the entrance of our apartment. By the time we got inside, he was yelling very loudly, and halfway up the first flight of steps, he lay down and refused to go any farther unless he could visit Grandma Elsa. He had still been somewhat of a nice little boy on the way in, closing the car door for me and opening the apartment door to get inside.

The argument was "Mommy, let's see Grandma Elsa."
I replied with, "We will see Grandma Elsa on Sunday."
"No, I want to see her now."

"We can't go now; it's late, and Grandma will be in bed soon."

"I want to see Grandma Elsa right now." And his voice was screeching as he lay in the middle of the steps.

I finally caved and said, "Yes, we will go to Grandma's house as soon as the groceries are put away." I thought the screaming would be easier to deal with inside my apartment rather than out in the wide-open echoing stairwell for the whole apartment complex to hear. He sounded like I was beating him half to death.

My little white lie worked, and he proceeded up the steps. I thought once I got him to the apartment, I could convince him we couldn't go and get him to bed. I was very wrong. He cried and screamed and carried on. I gave into my toddler's very first tantrum. "Oh boy," I thought. "This was not fun."

I told him I would call Grandma and ask if we could visit tonight and he could talk to her. "If she's going to bed, we'll have to stay home."

"*No, no, no!*" was his response.

I dialed Grandma's number, and I thought, "If she tells him no, he would be more understanding." Grandma answered, and I told her what was going on and asked if she minded some company in an hour for just a little while. We wouldn't stay long as it would be late when we got there.

"Oh yes" was the surprising response I got. She wasn't going to bed early tonight because there was a basketball game on that she couldn't miss so she would for sure be awake. She reminded me that we couldn't come visit on Sunday because she wasn't going to be home. She was headed to a birthday party for my great-uncle in Minnesota.

So off we went on a forty-five-mile trip to visit Grandma Elsa in the middle of the week.

Ethan ran into the house as fast as his little legs could carry him and threw his arms around Grandma's neck and held on like he would never see her again. It was long past everyone's bedtime when we finally left. Ethan gave Grandma another hug, and she said to him, "I'm glad you came to visit. You can't come visit this old grandma this weekend because I'm going to Jean's. It's Bob's birthday, and he wants to see this old grandma too." She pointed to the pictures on the hutch in the corner of the living room to show him who Jean and Bob were.

He blew her kisses at the door, and we left.

That was the last time we would see Grandma Elsa. On Friday morning of that week, the phone rang around seven in the morning. Grandma had passed away sometime that morning while packing for her weekend trip.

I didn't know how to explain a death to a two-year-old. I knew I would have to tell him something immediately after he woke up because he would wonder why I was crying. Grandma was his favorite person, and now she was gone.

Just as predicted, the moment he opened his eyes, he asked, "Why are you sad, Mommy?"

I told him Grandma passed away, and we wouldn't be able to see her anymore.

"Is she staying at Jean and Bob's? Why can't we go there?"

"Grandma didn't go to Jean and Bob's; she went to heaven instead."

"Where is heaven? Can we go there?"

"No, we can't."

"Why not?"

"Because it's so far away that no one can go there until God comes and takes us there."

"Who is God?"

"That's who is in charge of everything, and he comes to get everyone when it is their special time."

"Oh. Will I go there too and see Grandma?"

"Someday, but not for a very, very long time."

And with that he asked no more questions for the time being.

The questions started again when we attended the funeral.

"Why is Grandma in that box? Is she sleeping in there? Wake her up, Mom." He asked when he could see Grandma again and again through most of the summer, and then he just stopped.

A few months had passed since Grandma's passing, and summer was in full swing. We still kept our every-other-week routine of going home on Sundays. The only thing different was we didn't go to Grandma Elsa's anymore. We spent a little extra time at Grandma Agnes's house. To fill our time after that visit, we had many extra fishing adventures, trips to the zoo, and hours in the park. It was strange to drive by Grandma's house and not stop, but we managed.

"There's Grandma's house, right, Mom?"

"Yep."

"But she doesn't live there anymore 'cause she lives in heaven, right, Mom?"

"Right."

When the summer came to an end and school started again, our routine changed just a little to accommodate my new school schedule. Ethan started going to a new day care that he absolutely loved and got a new at-home babysitter because his dad changed jobs and had a different work schedule. He adjusted well to the new routine. Once fall rolled around, he started feeling ill off and on, with a couple of ear infections with fevers and lots of extra napping. Nothing we were too concerned about. We went about our daily life, with just the occasional antibiotic on board.

CHAPTER 6

A Visit from Grandma

* * *

ETHAN SPENT THE FIRST WEEK of October going back and forth between grandmas and babysitters. He wasn't able to go to day care because he had an ear infection that was accompanied by a low-grade temp. I took him to the walk-in clinic at the beginning of the week because of his fever, and they found an ear infection in just one ear to be the cause. I still had to go to school and work, so instead of calling in sick, I toted him around between grandmas and sitters. He didn't mind. He loved going to day care, but he also loved visiting other people. Even though he was sick, he didn't act or appear to be. He was still his happy, bubbly, social self and carried on like normal. The only difference in his daily routine was the antibiotic he had to take morning and night and his not being able to attend day care.

On the eve of my birthday, October 7, 2001, I sat down on the couch after work to study. I was home alone. I had fallen asleep where I sat. I suddenly woke up from a noise in the entryway. I stood up, startled and a bit scared. I thought the door was locked, and I swear I heard it slam shut—that was the reason for my sudden jolt awake. As I went slowly around the corner to see what the noise was from and who might be there, Grandma Elsa approached me, smiling. Not two steps behind her was my mom's cousin Sharon.

"What are you doing here?" I asked, happy but confused. Surely this was a very vivid dream. Grandma had been gone for six months, Sharon much longer.

Grandma, still smiling, said, "You didn't think we'd forget your birthday, did you?"

Oh yeah, it was my birthday. After such a busy, stressful week, I had forgotten my own birthday. Twenty-one was a birthday to be celebrated, and I'd forgotten. How do you forget you're turning twenty-one? I had been waiting for this birthday since the beginning of time.

Grandma and Sharon had stopped by just to wish me a happy birthday. Grandma was dressed in a burgundy blazer and black pants. Sharon was in a pink sweater and light-colored blue jeans.

Just as fast as they were there, I shot straight up on the couch, and they were gone. Sleeping. Dreaming. Anatomy and physiology notes still in my lap. *Nick at Night* was playing on the TV. I looked behind me, and no one was there. I got up to make sure the door was locked and took myself to bed. "What a weird dream," I thought. A nice dream, but weird. It had seemed so real. Grandma never forgot a birthday, and I must have been missing her to have such a vivid dream.

The next morning, when I rolled out of bed, I had such a good, warm feeling about my almost-as-real-as-life dream that I had to call my mom and tell her about it. She was one to believe in ghosts and angels and the great afterlife. Even though I had experienced an angel myself many years ago, I was still somewhat of a skeptic. I knew my mom would love to hear about my dream, and I just had to tell someone who wouldn't think I was completely nuts.

"Oh, Jennifer, Grandma was there to wish you a happy birthday."

Mom wanted to keep talking about it, but I didn't have much time to think about it or analyze it over the phone. I had to get to class and head to work right after. I also had to line up a backup babysitter just in case my little man didn't make it through the day without spiking a temp. What a week! He was at his grandma's with his dad, and his dad was dropping him off at day care on his way to work that morning. I was also hoping his fever would be nice so I could experience barhopping for the first time.

CHAPTER 7

The Horrible Month of October

*   *   *

I MADE IT THROUGH THE school day on my birthday. I also made it to work. I wasn't two hours into my eight-hour shift when I was paged overhead for a phone call. I was not surprised at all to hear my day-care provider on the other end. I was expecting him to tell me that Ethan had a fever, again, but he did not.

"Jen."

"Yeah."

"I don't really know what to tell you here, but something really weird is going on with Ethan."

"Like what?"

"Well…I don't think he has a fever today, but when he got up from his nap, his whole face was swollen. Is he allergic to anything?" And he proceeded to rattle off everything he ate for breakfast and lunch. He wasn't allergic to anything that I was aware of yet, but maybe he'd developed an allergy. "He also has some red spots all over his eyes, and his eyes are so puffy it looks like he can't even see. Are you able to come and get him? I guess he is okay here, but I'd really feel more comfortable if you'd come and pick him up."

"Okay, I'll be there shortly. If I can't leave, I'll have someone else bring him here."

"Okay, thanks."

I was able to leave work and pick him up within thirty minutes. The day-care provider wasn't kidding when he said something weird was going on. My kid didn't even look like my kid. His whole face was swollen, and he looked like a completely different child than the one I had seen the day before. His day-care provider said he looked perfectly normal when he got there that morning. He ate lunch, took a nap, and woke up looking like this. I was shocked.

I drove him directly to the walk-in clinic to be seen. Luckily his own pediatrician was the doctor in the walk-in clinic that day. He wasn't sure what was going on but suspected it was from the ear infection. He ran some blood tests, checked his ears, and prescribed some steroids to minimize the swelling. When the results of the blood test came back, there was just a slight elevation in his white blood count. He was still on an antibiotic for an ear infection, which seemed to be going away. He was to take the steroids for five days and come back to the clinic in a week. We went out for supper after the clinic and played some arcade games.

Once we got home, it was time for medicine and bed. Ethan plopped up on the counter right next to the microwave, where he liked to take his medicine, and waited for me to measure out the doses. He started with the not-so-bad-tasting pink one and then moved on to the horrible other pink one. We didn't know it was horrible until he put it in his mouth. His whole body shivered, and I thought he was going to toss up his supper right there on the kitchen floor. "It can't be that bad," I thought. When he was done shivering from the wicked taste, he ran off to the bathroom to get ready for bed.

I was able to go out later that evening to celebrate my once-in-a-lifetime birthday. I didn't whoop it up too good and somewhat disappointed my coworkers, but I was so tired and slightly worried about Ethan. I had a great time, but it wasn't the epic birthday celebration I had anticipated for most of my life.

The next day Ethan seemed to be doing better. We had to force the steroids down his throat because of the horrible taste, and I felt like a child abuser, but they worked. The swelling went away. We went to the clinic the following week, and everything seemed to have cleared up. We left thinking the illness was behind us.

The following evening things changed again. As Ethan was standing on his step stool brushing his teeth, I noticed lumps on the side of his neck. Very large and visible when he turned his head to the side to talk to me and unseen when he was facing the mirror. I asked him to turn and look at me, and the lumps appeared just like marbles under his skin.

"Look in the mirror," I told him, and they disappeared. I had him get down from the stool, and I felt the side of his neck. I could feel the little hard knobs under his skin. "Do these hurt?" I asked him.

"Nope." And he hopped back up to continue brushing his teeth.

The following day we headed right back to the walk-in clinic. Swollen lymph nodes because of yet another infection in the ear. White blood count: fifteen thousand. Not much over the normal range. We went home with another ten days of antibiotics. We scheduled yet another follow-up appointment for the next week before we left.

After a couple of days of the antibiotics, the swollen lymph nodes were gone. While we were waiting for the week to pass and the illness to leave us, we learned that my cousin, who was also my go-to weekend babysitter, was in the hospital with the Epstein-Barr virus. A nasty form of mononucleosis. For sure this is what Ethan had. She watched him all summer long after day-care hours and every other weekend when I had to work. Mono is contagious, and they shared a bottle of Mountain Dew every time she was there. Mystery solved.

I mentioned this to his pediatrician during our follow-up visit the next week. More blood tests were run, and no mono. The ear infection seemed to still be hanging on, so we kept up with the antibiotics and were to return again the following week. We were now on week four of ear infection and mystery symptoms.

I was missing a lot of school and had to cover some of my work shifts to stay home with Ethan. He went to stay at my mom's for the weekend so I could work a couple of full days and get caught up on homework. He went home with her when she got off work on Friday evening, and she was going to drop him off early Monday morning on her way back to work. His next clinic appointment was Monday afternoon.

CHAPTER 8

A Second Visit from Grandma

✳   ✳   ✳

GRANDMA CAME TO VISIT AGAIN. Exactly twenty-one days after her first visit. Unlike the first visit, this one left me with a terrible, uneasy feeling. It was much the same as the first time she was there. I had fallen asleep on the couch with books in my lap and the TV going. I figured again that I was dreaming. I just had to be, but the feeling this dream left me with was one I couldn't describe.

In this dream, I was startled awake by the sound of the door. I turned around to see who was there. I stood from the couch and turned the corner through my kitchen on my way to the door. There inside my kitchen stood Grandma Elsa. This time she was alone. She was dressed in the same burgundy blazer and black pants. She was smiling, but with her smile, there was a look of seriousness and concern.

"What are you doing here?" I asked her.

She replied with, "I'm taking Ethan."

"What do you mean, you're taking Ethan? Taking him where?"

"You just never mind. Just listen to this old lady. I'm taking Ethan, and he'll be all right."

And just as suddenly as she'd appeared, the door shut with a loud slam. I jolted straight up from my sleep and sat straight up. The feeling in my gut said that wasn't a dream. Grandma was just standing in my kitchen having the oddest conversation with me. If it wasn't a dream, why was I still sitting on my couch? I hurried through the kitchen, unbolted the door lock, and swung the door open so I could catch her or someone in my hallway. Someone had just slammed my apartment door. If not Grandma, then who was it? I headed down the hall, trying not to run. I busted into my friend's apartment and wanted to know if he was just in my kitchen.

He looked at me, confused, and gave me a solid, honest, "No, I haven't left this couch all night."

I turned and walked back to my own apartment and stood in the kitchen for what felt like forever. As I stood there, thinking that my friend was lying and actually was there just minutes ago, I spotted my spare key placed right in front of the toaster. He couldn't have been in here. The key he uses was here, and you can't lock the dead bolt from the outside without it. I turned and looked around some, and then I noticed the smell. My whole kitchen and the entrance to my apartment were filled with the scent of Grandma Elsa's favorite perfume. Then I was scared.

The uneasy gut feeling I had that something was wrong turned into fear and panic. It was just around two in the morning, but I picked up the phone and dialed my parents' house, where Ethan was staying for the weekend. My mom answered the phone.

"Is Ethan okay?" I asked. My voice was trembling, along with the rest of my body.

"He's just fine, Jen. What is wrong?"

I was very near tears as I told her that Grandma Elsa was just here. "I feel like I was dreaming, but I swear I wasn't. I can smell her. Like she was just standing right here. She told me she was taking Ethan."

"Ethan is just fine."

"I don't think he is. I'm going to come and pick him up."

My mom convinced me that I was being ridiculous and that I should go back to bed, and she would bring him home as soon as he woke up. I was nervous about it, but I agreed that yes, maybe I was being a bit ridiculous, but I couldn't shake the feeling that something was wrong, I just didn't know what.

Just as promised, Mom delivered Ethan just before noon the next day. He was perfectly fine for the time being. We all ran a couple of errands around town for a few hours and headed to Applebee's for a late lunch.

CHAPTER 9

Cancer

* * *

We returned home from our late lunch and all-day shopping adventures. Ethan left the restaurant with a helium balloon. He was so excited all the way home, shaking his balloon around in the back seat and giggling. When we pulled into the apartment parking lot and got out of the car, he let his balloon go and giggled and squealed as it blew higher and higher in the wind. I noticed in the sunlight that he looked pale and had dark circles under his little eyes. He was in good spirits, so I assumed he was sporting his "I have been sick for a month" look, and this was probably normal. He bounced all the way up the stairs to our apartment, and when we got inside, I instructed him to get ready for a bath, and we would hang out on the couch and watch cartoons until bedtime.

He ran to the bathroom to start his bathwater while I grabbed jammies and a diaper. He met me in the hallway to help remove his clothes. He ripped off his shirt and tossed it in the laundry basket and then plopped down in front of me to help him with his pants and diaper. He wasn't wearing diapers during the day anymore, but today I convinced him to put one on because we were out and about all day, and I didn't want him to have an accident. He lifted his legs straight up in the air, and as I grabbed the bottom of his pants and tugged straight up as I always do, he let out a bloodcurdling scream. It was a scream of pain. He wiggled away from me so fast; he banged his head on the wall and was instantly on his feet.

"My belly hurts, Mom. It hurts real bad." He walked into the bathroom, and in the bright light while he was turned to the side, I could see his belly. It protruded out so far that he looked like one of those malnourished kids you see on TV commercials. I lifted him up to help him into the tub, and then the vomit came. So fast and so hard it splashed on the wall across the room with force. Everything he ate all day, and it just kept coming at the same speed and force for several minutes. I knew once bath time was over, after just enough time to clean up the vomit, we were headed straight to the emergency department.

I thought back to the time when I was infected with mono and was sick for six months before I had a diagnosis and my spleen was so swollen I had to stay in bed for two weeks. I thought that's what this was. He had an appointment in the clinic the next day, but we were going to the ER. I called my mom and asked her if she'd noticed any swelling in his belly the night before, and she hadn't. He was just fine. I told her we were going to the ER; she said she was going to turn around and meet us there.

We arrived at the ER, and a nurse escorted us to a small room directly across from the nurse's station. We went over Ethan's illnesses for the past month. The ear infection, the mystery fevers, the extra napping, the waking up at night with pain in his legs, the red dots on his eyes, the swelling of his face. Every week he had a new and different ailment. Just like clockwork. Once a week, every week, for exactly four weeks, and now here we were with these new symptoms. I told her about his exposure to the mono.

While we were waiting for the on-call pediatrician to arrive, they started an IV and checked his vitals. He was okay with the IV. At this point, he was a professional with blood draws, having had so many in the last month. He wasn't okay with the pulse oximeter they wrapped around his big toe. He acted like it was a monster that was about to swallow him whole, starting at his feet.

The doctor came in, chatted with us, and told us what kinds of things he was looking for in his blood work; he said he would be back to let us know what the results were just as soon as he got them back. He disappeared into the hallway.

I was watching the comings and goings of the ER staff from my chair. Ethan was content. Talking up a storm, playing with trucks, and sucking a lollipop. He got his sucker for being such a good sport with his IV insertion.

I was thinking this might be the place I wanted to work when I got done with school in a couple of years. Always busy, always exciting, and always something new. I was trying to distract myself from what was going on. My little boy was sick, we didn't know why, and I was already tired of it.

It wasn't long after they took Ethan's blood that I noticed the doctor take a seat at the desk in front of me. He seemed to be making notes. He said a few words to a couple of nurses who were going back and forth. I couldn't hear what they were saying, but after he talked to them, he got up and left. I thought to myself it wasn't us he was talking about because no one came into our room. Surely there was more than one child in the ER that night. It was busy. The whole place was packed.

Within a few minutes, I started to notice the looks. Every person who walked by our room after the doctor left looked in at us like they felt sorry for us. It was an "oh, that poor kid" look. On every single face! I felt like a young teen again, having the feeling that all eyes are on me. Was I being paranoid? I didn't think so, so I alerted my parents to take a look and see what they thought. I told them, "I think something is very wrong here. Look at everyone who walks by. Do they all have sympathetic looks when they glance in here?" I was not paranoid; they noticed it too. I felt like we were about to get some very bad news. The looks carried on for more than twenty minutes.

The doctor was back at the desk again, this time toting a manila envelope. He sat for a minute in front of the computer. He got up, picked up his envelope, and headed in our direction with that sympathetic look on his face. I could see him take a deep breath when he walked through the door. It was a sigh like "this is the part of my job that I hate, but I have to do it."

"Can we go somewhere private to talk?" Those dreaded words that I heard for the first time. I could feel all my insides rise into my throat. I've watched enough television in my life to know that whatever he had to say wasn't going to be good. They never tell you the good news in private. "The nurse will stay with Ethan, and we will be back in a few minutes. I want all of you to come, not just Mom."

Oh God, what was he about to tell us? My entire body was trembling as he led us past the nurse's station and around the corner to a tiny little room. We all picked a chair and tightly sat surrounding the doctor. My mouth was completely dry, and everything was shaking. Fight or flight. I wanted to run. There was ringing in my ears. I think I wished it there myself so I didn't have to hear what he had to say.

"I do have some bad news. The blood work seems to reveal that your son has some type of leukemia."

The ringing in my ears turned up to a dull roar. Leukemia is cancer, and that's all I knew. And because I knew nothing of leukemia or any type of cancer, the only thing in my brain was death.

The doctor seemed to be able to read my thoughts, as his next words were "Cancer doesn't mean a death sentence. We have to determine exactly what type of leukemia it is, and we will go from there. I have called in our pediatric oncologist, and she is on her way to discuss all the details of what's to come with you. I have also called in Ethan's pediatrician, and he is on his way. For now, we will get you situated in a room and prepare you to stay the night. The oncologist will meet you when you get settled in. I'm sure you have many questions that the oncologist is far more qualified to answer."

I felt the tears start to trickle down my face. They were just hanging out in my eyes during the whole conversation, and now they fell. And there were many. I kept repeating to myself in my head, "This is not a death sentence." Comforting words to repeat to yourself when your baby has cancer. I needed a minute to regroup and to put on my warrior face. I had to regroup the group. No crying! Absolutely no crying in front of Ethan. This is no doubt going to be the worst and scariest thing he'll ever experience, and he doesn't need all of us crying to get scared before it starts to get really scary.

The doctor on call went over the blood work with us and briefly explained how leukemia grows and what it does in the body when it circulates through the bloodstream. He told us that had we waited until his scheduled clinic visit in the morning, we might have been too late. Ethan most likely would have to start treatment soon, maybe even tonight. His white blood count went from fifteen thousand earlier that week to slightly over one hundred eighty thousand. There was a good chance that with the rough movements of a toddler, his spleen or liver could easily have ruptured from the overwhelming amount of extra white blood cells passing through. We would likely be transferred from this hospital to a larger one, where pediatric kidney dialysis was available.

After what seemed like forever, we finally made it to our room and waited for the oncologist to arrive. Our pediatrician was there and explained many things to us. He seemed to be just as devastated at the news as we were. Going over the symptoms and why we didn't see this or suspect that because really, who thinks about cancer in a two-year-old? We didn't. None of us did. It seemed to come out of nowhere, and it pretty much did. His white blood count wasn't much above the normal range just a few days earlier.

I explained to Ethan, in the best way I could, in two-year-old terms, what was about to happen to him. We used plastic bugs for some animation. "Your blood is made up of tiny little bugs that swim around in your veins." I pointed at some veins that were visible and told him that's what his IV was sticking in. "Most of the bugs in your blood are good bugs, but sometimes bad bugs get in there. When bad bugs get in there, there are superbugs that beat up all the bad bugs and chase them out. That's what is happening in your body when you feel sick. All the superbugs are having a fight with the bad guys. Your superbugs got sick and they have no one to help them, so you're going to need to get a lot of medicine for a very long time to make the superbugs feel better again. You're going to feel sick a lot while all the bugs are trying to get better. Lots of shots and blood draws and icky medicine to get rid of the bugs." He was okay with the explanation, and before all the bad stuff started, he was even excited. His body was going to war with some bad bugs that he couldn't see, and he and the good bugs were going to be superheroes.

When the oncologist arrived and explained in more detail what the next many years of our lives were going to be like, it seemed like a blur. We would be packing up and moving to Minneapolis for at least the next month and maybe longer, depending on how Ethan responded to his first course of treatment. The treatment after the first week would be decided by a team of oncologists at the University of Minnesota and would be based on what type of leukemia he had. The immediate plan was to have a bone marrow biopsy in the morning, ride an ambulance to the airport, and board a plane that would fly us right to Minneapolis. Another ambulance would collect us there and drive us to the hospital.

Ethan was baptized by our local pastor in his hospital bed early the next morning. Not something I was concerned about, but some of our grandmothers said it was necessary. Soon after the short ceremony, he was wheeled into a treatment room around the corner from his room for his bone marrow biopsy. I wasn't allowed to be in there during the procedure but stayed with him until he was lightly sedated and the doctor was ready to begin. I wasn't comfortable leaving him during something so unpleasant, but it was the first of many unpleasant experiences that we would have to get used to.

I thought I was prepared, but I was not. I stood outside the room, as close as they would allow. I could hear the doctor explain what she was going to do and that it was going to hurt, but she would do it as fast as she could so it wouldn't hurt for long. That's when the scream came and he begged for his mom. I couldn't imagine the pain, but I could hear it in my child's voice. This was just the beginning. And for the first time since we got there, I really cried. Tears ran from my face, and I sobbed. Why does something so horrible have to happen to someone so small? Someone who can't even fully understand the awfulness that he was about to endure for the next few years ahead of him. It wasn't fair, and I wanted to trade places with him.

Because everything happened so fast and it was into the middle of the night on Sunday when we wrapped things up and had an action plan, it was decided that my mom would fly with Ethan to the city for him to begin his treatment. She and my dad were scheduled to take a cruise for their anniversary that week, so they had no responsibilities for the next two weeks and now no cruise to go on. Ethan's dad and I were both due to go to work Monday, he in the morning and I in the afternoon. I also had classes to attend in the morning. We had many things to take care of and people to tell before we interrupted our lives for the next months. Mom would fly there, and we would come behind that evening in the car. Ethan would have to be sedated for the first part of his treatment, so he wouldn't miss us. We would arrive sometime that evening.

To make things quick and easy for us, sometime during the night, we just typed up a generic note and made several copies. Inconvenient maybe for the recipients, but short and effective to let them know. "Sorry for the inconvenience; our son was diagnosed with cancer last night. We're leaving town for one month to begin his treatment immediately. We'll call next week when we have more details. Thank you for understanding." We signed our names, with a date underneath.

There was so much paper work to fill out. We had to sign so many documents for my mom to fly with him. They were all so she could make medical decisions in our absence. It was likely that treatment would have to start as soon as they arrived at the hospital, and with his dad and I packing up and driving there, it would be several hours difference when we got there. What if something happens on the flight? What if he needs a breathing tube? What if he needs CPR? Do I trust my mom to decide those things for my son on my behalf? "All stupid questions," I thought, but realistic I guessed.

I rode with Ethan in the ambulance to the airport. He was pretty excited to get on a plane and fly somewhere. He was also excited that his grandma was going with him. We had a little talk on the way about getting medicine when he got there and how everything might hurt, but he should be good for the doctors because they were trying to help him get rid of the bad bugs in his blood. I explained that his dad and I were going to come in the car because we had to pack stuff to stay there for a really long time. He was okay with his grandma staying with him until the nighttime. I told him that he would probably get some medicine that would make him really sleepy, and we would probably be there when he woke up.

The day went so fast, yet it seemed to drag on forever. We both stopped at our workplaces, dropped off our notes where we were able, packed bags and a few of Ethan's favorite things, dropped off the cat with our parents, and hit the road. A quick stop for gas at Grandma's gas station, and she sent us off with snacks and a fistful of money. We'd only been cancer parents for a few hours, but word travels fast in a small town, and already people in our community were giving us money to help with the extra expenses. It was a really nice surprise. We would soon learn how expensive it was to eat away from home every single day.

CHAPTER 10

Our New Experience

* * *

I STARED OUT THE WINDOW almost the whole trip. I didn't have much to say, and my mind was just blank. How does this happen? How can a perfectly healthy little boy just get out of bed one day and be full of cancer? The drive seemed to take forever. We turned up the radio a few times to listen to a few good songs and clear our heads. There are some songs that today I cannot listen to because they remind me of that day my kid got cancer.

It was late when we arrived at the hospital. After normal visiting hours. We were greeted in the main entrance by a very large security guard. Already nervous wrecks, we had to endure over one hundred questions and a pat down just to get to the elevator. What's your name? Why are you here? Show your ID; give us your license plate number, blood type, last meal, height, and weight. It wasn't really that bad, but way too many questions. So very irritating. The man was only doing his job and keeping the hospital staff and patients safe, but at that particular moment, punching him right in the throat seemed so delightful to me. I came to grow very fond of him soon after our first encounter, and we even missed him a little when we left there, but that night, he was not my favorite.

After no less than twenty minutes of questioning, we were armed with our bright-green "parent" badge and pointed in the direction of unit 5B. Our new home away from home. Our walk to the elevator was a slow one because we weren't completely sure where to go, so stopping to read all the signs on the way was a must. The place was very big. It was decorated nicely and smelled of coffee and something else I couldn't pinpoint. We finally spotted the elevators. Six total. Three on each wall and very big. When we got to the fifth floor, the hallway branched in three different directions. A whole new set of smells to get used to and a whole new level of places to get lost.

I talked to my mom off and on through the whole trip, and she kept us updated on what was happening and what was going to happen. Her explanation and the doctor's explanations did not even come close to prepare me for what I was about to find when I entered Ethan's hospital room for the first time.

CHAPTER 11

Our Journey with Cancer–The First Month

* * *

I OPENED THE DOOR TO Ethan's room. There was a weird noise coming from somewhere inside. It smelled funny, and I could see my mom standing over a really tall crib. I was hoping to be greeted by my smiley little boy when I could see around the corner. Instead, I was greeted by a giant machine, and things from that moment are permanently burned into my brain that forever changed me.

Lying on the bed was not my happy, bubbly, little boy, but a lifeless, frail child with tubes coming from everywhere tubes could possibly come from. In addition to the IV coming from his arm was an oxygen tube in his nose, a pulse oximeter on his toe, a blood pressure cuff on his arm, and two very large tubes stuck into the top of each leg and secured down with what seemed like an entire roll of very strange-looking tape. There was a very large machine sitting in the left corner of the room. Things were spinning. There was a whooshing, sucking noise that sounded rhythmically every couple of seconds. The machine was attached to the hoses that seemed to be larger than the tiny little legs they were attached to. Ethan looked sick. I was sick at the sight of him. All the sounds and the scary sights and smells had my head spinning. It seemed like only thirty seconds had passed for me to take it all in when I was greeted by a team of pediatric oncologists.

After the initial shock of all the machines and an explanation of what was to come, we tried to settle into our new home and adjust to our new life. Ethan was sedated for the first couple of days. We managed to find a cheap hotel for most of us to crash in as there was room for only one at Ethan's bedside, and the waiting rooms were a bit crowded and not at all comfortable. The local Ronald McDonald house put us on a waiting list, and we would be notified as soon as they had a room for us.

The giant machine in the corner of his room was "washing" his blood. Blood was removed from his body by the tube in one leg and sent into the machine. The machine would somehow remove white blood cells, and then the blood was returned to his body through the tube in his other leg. Two days after the process of washing the blood started, they decided to lighten Ethan's sedation. His white blood count dropped a great deal, and they needed to get his port placed to begin his treatments. Some drugs were already being administered, but it was dangerous to put them into the IV for long periods of time.

Upon waking up, Ethan was starving. He didn't understand anything that was going on, even though we explained things to him as best we could before we arrived. Like us, the explanations didn't come close to preparing him for the reality of it all. "Why are these tubes in my legs?" "Get that thing off my toe." "Why can't I walk?" "Let's go home." "I want teddy-bear cookies." "Get me chicken nuggets." "Get this thing off my toe." "My head is on fire." All the questions and small demands that were so simple, yet impossible and devastating. Trying to explain to a two-year-old why he couldn't have anything to eat when he was so hungry was horrible. You can't walk because all these tubes are here to save your life. You can't take that monitor off your toe, because what if? The drugs he was getting were making his head hot, and he insisted there was a fire in his hair. He kept tugging at the hair on top of his head, telling us to put out the fire. He begged for food, begged to take all the tubes and monitors out, and begged to go home. It was so hard to stay strong and hold it together, but we had to, so he could hold it together and get through the next three years.

We moved into our regular hospital room on day three. Room 535 on unit 5B. Our new home. The place where we would reside for a whole month. One month isn't a long time, but it seemed like forever. Ethan's port was placed. It was just a temporary one that would stay put until closer to his discharge date, when a more permanent one would be put in. He wasn't going to see outside of the hospital wall for twenty-eight days. This temporary one was suitable until we were ready to go home.

Ethan adjusted to his new homelife a little better than we did. He had a pretty good view of the river and had taken the guest chair as his own. He parked it in front of the window so he could watch the boats go by while he watched movies, played PlayStation, and ordered snacks on demand from the hospital staff. He was an expert at ringing the nurse whenever he needed a new game, movie, or snack. He made fast friends with all the hospital staff with his infectious giggle and big, sparkly, bright-blue eyes.

It didn't take long for our room to fill up with cards and gifts. The extralarge picture window was soon filled with cards; Ethan insisted they all hang so he could look at them every day. We had to be careful not to block his view of the river, but the cards all had to be hung. Stuck there with bulky white pieces of hospital tape. Ethan was depressed in the first couple of weeks as he adjusted to his new normal. He had a hard time understanding why we wouldn't take him home. In his two-year-old mind, he was convinced that he did something wrong and was being punished for something.

After doing the same thing every day for the first two years of his life, we had to do new things every day. Most days were the same, but there were so many new things to learn and adjust to. Going anywhere without an IV pole was a thing of the past. There was almost never any freedom from that thing. Always a tube hung from his chest that would drag between his legs with every step he would take. He learned really fast not to step on it, and everyone who visited was instructed to watch out for his tubies. He developed a funny little limp so as not to step on his tubies when he was running around the room. Bath time, which was the best part of the day at home and happened every night, was now like a vacation for him that came only once or twice a week. He could take a bath only when there was freedom from drugs and fluids and only after a nurse taped up, with several pounds of plastic and a few rolls of tape, the tube that came out of his chest. The chance of infection in the blood was great.

When the first two weeks of treatment were over, we were given a little more freedom to leave our room and explore the hospital a bit. Trips to the pop machine and the cafeteria for Coke and snacks were an everyday adventure, unless blood counts were too low. We walked to the pop machine and rode in a wagon to the cafeteria. There never was a trip in the wagon without his purple people eater. Ethan received this gift from a friend and didn't leave the room without it. There were very few people who rode an elevator with us who weren't convinced to dance to "The Purple People Eater" song. It was necessary before every little treatment that took place, even just checking a temperature, for the hospital staff to dance. Some of the regular staff just started dancing upon entering the room before the song even played. He would giggle every time. Everyone left Ethan feeling a bit happier than when they came in. Even on his grumpy days, the purple people eater made him smile, and grumpy days came often, especially on steroid days.

Our days in the hospital started to pass a little faster the longer we were there. Once we got the hang of things and everything wasn't new anymore, it was just normal everyday life. Ethan always had visitors every week to help pass the time. There was mail every day. Oh my! Was there mail! The mail always came with treats, toys, money, and sometimes just letters from strangers. He loved the mail! Sometimes our visitors included Snoopy the dog, Ronald McDonald, and various other characters. Ethan's favorite day was Sunday. Once he figured out that he could see the Viking stadium from his room and everyone who worked here loved the Vikings, he proudly sported his Packers attire and showed off to the whole hospital. Every Sunday there were fights and bets among Ethan and the hospital staff over who had the better team and who was going to win that day.

When the second two weeks of the treatment started, Ethan's hair began to fall out. Not much at first. We noticed it in the bathtub. Chunks of his thick light-brown hair would be stuck everywhere. Once it started to fall out, he would sit in his favorite green chair by the window and pull his hair out by the handfuls and make a pile on the bedside table. No one was allowed to throw it away. "That's my hair!" he would yell if anyone came close to it. He received a container of homemade cookies in the mail, and when he was sick and tired of everyone trying to move or throw away his hair collection, he dumped those cookies in the garbage and put his pile of hair in the cookie container. He continued to collect his hair until there wasn't a single one left on his head. He gave himself the name "Q-ball" and told everyone he passed that he was a q-ball now because he had bugs in his blood and everyone should refer to him as such. To date, we have a Rubbermaid container of Ethan's full head of hair, minus what washed down the bathtub drain, plus a dozen or so cookie crumbs that remained in the bottom of the container.

We made it to week three without any complications. Ethan was considered to be in remission, and plans for discharge were underway. They scheduled a time to have his IV line removed and a more permanent port put in place. By the time we got to week three, Ethan was an expert on his drugs and treatments. When the port was placed, he had a lot more freedom from his IV pole and no longer had tubes dangling around all the time. The little limp he developed to avoid stepping on the tubes remained out of habit, even when the line was no longer there.

The worst thing we had to tackle before our trip home was swallowing the oral meds. The prednisone he had to take before the cancer diagnosis ruined him for taking liquid medication ever again. We thought of every trick in the book to get those meds in him, and our little, smarter-than-us two-year-old wouldn't fall for any of them. We bribed him, took things away, even faked our own kidnapping by monsters, and he wasn't budging. Dissolving the meds in his Coke, putting them in his food, sneaking them in anywhere, he caught us every time. He was more than happy to sit in dark silence and starve to death if he didn't have to take that medicine. We told him we couldn't go home until he took the pills or the liquid, but he didn't care. He thought this was where we lived now anyway, and he was happy and content just living in the hospital forever.

He finally decided on a random day out of nowhere that he was ready. Maybe he finally believed we were really going to go home and leave him there by himself and take all his stuff with us, because we might have told him that once or twice. He just popped each pill in his mouth and washed them down with a swallow of Coke and just casually pushed the pill cup in the garbage. He didn't look at any of us, just stared at the TV. We didn't even get a cocky "watch and learn," which was his favorite thing to tell us when he did something new. Just casual, like it was normal everyday stuff that he'd been doing for years.

CHAPTER 12

Going Home

*   *   *

THE DAY FOR US TO return home finally arrived, and much
to our surprise, Ethan didn't actually want to leave. After
a couple of weeks of being there, he stopped asking to go
to day care and to his apartment. Everyone was there to
visit, so he just thought this was our new home. It took us
forever to pack. He had accumulated so much stuff in the
month we were there. One full car, one full pickup, and
the back seat of another car were stuffed with gifts that
filled our hospital room. So much stuff we almost had to
strap Ethan to the roof of the car just to get his things
home. He would have gladly ridden that way too if it meant
all his new belongings would get home safely. We even had
a live fish to tote home!

Ethan was reluctant to pack his things. "Where are
you going with this?" "What are you doing with that?"

"Home."

"To our apartment?"

"Yes."

"The one in Bismarck?"

"Yes."

He questioned it like this was our apartment in Minneapolis and we had another one in Bismarck.

"Are we leaving Minnionapples?"

"Yes."

"Are we coming back tomorrow?"

"No."

"Why are we leaving?"

"You can get the rest of your medicine at home."

"When can we come back?"

"Sometime, but not for a while."

I had to remind him of all the things he was going home to. All the things he begged for the first week we were here, which he seemed now to have forgotten.

"Oh" was his response, and the same questions were on repeat almost the entire ride home.

We drove away from the hospital with comfort, knowing that the worst part of this long journey was behind us. Or so we thought at the time. I was relieved, Ethan was anxious, but we were going home. Home to find another new normal for the next few years.

CHAPTER 13

Our New Life—The Clinic Life

* * *

Our new routine started almost immediately when we got home. We had the weekend to breathe and get ready, and then it was off to the clinic at eight o'clock Monday morning.

Every Monday morning started with a routine blood draw to see what the blood cells were up to and if we could proceed with the drugs on schedule. Neutrophils were the important guys. Those were the cells that usually decided what was going to happen for the rest of the week. Most of the time they were good, and treatments proceeded as planned. Every once in a while, we got a much-needed break. Breaks were nice, but a break for the week just meant this would be prolonged for another week at the end of our treatment schedule.

Ethan adjusted very well to our new life. I struggled with it at times. He couldn't go to day care most of the time due to his increased risk of infection, so many nights were spent being juggled between friends and family so his dad and I could go to work occasionally. I wasn't able to work full time anymore, but I worked as much as I could.

We spent pretty much every day in the clinic, Monday through Thursday, having treatments, transfusions, blood draws, shots, vitals, everything. Our clinic visits usually ended on Thursday unless blood counts were low. Fridays were spent in either the clinic or the hospital when it was necessary. It was exhausting. Mondays and Thursdays were blood-draw days, and if things checked out on Mondays, there would be chemotherapy for the rest of the week. Sometimes that included an IV for the entire day, sometimes only an hour or two. Some days he just got a quick shot through his port or in his legs. Once a month there was intrathecal chemotherapy, and those days were tough. Always on a Monday. He would be sedated so the medication could be administered right into his spinal column. Intramuscular shot days were also rough because those went right into the leg muscle and burned so badly. Those were the days we dreaded. Ethan was okay with the poking and prodding at this point, but those days he feared. He screamed in pain for the leg shots, and most often some very colorful words came from his cute little toddler mouth. After a few months, he got used to the back shots and eventually didn't even need sedation for those. Other than those few bad days, he loved going to the clinic.

By the second week of going, he knew everyone working there by first name and never ran out of stories to tell everyone. He always wanted to know everyone's business and how their day was going. If someone was missing, he would question their whereabouts. On IV days he would hop into the Fisher-Price car, and I would have to follow behind and push his pole so he could scoot around the whole clinic and see what everyone was up to. "How was your weekend?" On a rare occasion, I could get him to settle down and watch a movie in the waiting room so I could catch a nap, but that didn't happen very often. His favorite thing to do was grab the doctor's plastic snakes and throw them at the nurses to scare them. He made so many new friends, not just with clinic staff but other patients as well. He also lost a couple of friends during the first year, which was very sad.

What we did with our time when we weren't at the clinic completely revolved around what was happening at the clinic or what treatments he was receiving. Monday's blood draw determined the course of treatment for the week, and Thursday's blood draw determined our weekend plans. We could never really plan anything in advance because we had to wait and see what the blood told us. If Thursday blood counts were low, we would have to stick around indoors and away from people so as not to catch an infection. Just a simple trip to Walmart or the grocery store was out of the question on a Saturday afternoon if his blood counts were too low. If we had to venture out into the public, he had to wear a mask, and he wanted nothing to do with that, so we had to stay home. How could he talk to every person he saw with his mouth covered? The thought of wearing a mask was just crazy to him.

More often than not, blood counts were good to us, and his first year of treatments was pretty adventurous. With all the different people he got to hang out with on weekends so I could go to work, he became a jack-of-all-trades and made dozens of new friends. He spent days at Grandma and Grandpa's gas station, where he hung out mostly in the shop to avoid any sick people. In the shop, he became an expert at changing oil and changing and balancing tires. Many days were spent at the farm, where he would fix fences; check cows; drive the tractor; and hunt gophers, rabbits, coyotes, and sometimes deer. There were so many fishing trips, and many days were spent with me at work, where he got to play all the arcade games he wanted for free. He got to help with some house-remodeling projects and hang out at the ambulance garage, where he often got to be a practice patient. During the summer months when we had to return to Minneapolis for cranial radiation, we spent hours and days at the Mall of America and made a couple of trips to Valley Fair.

The first year of treatment was a breeze. Ethan had zero days of ill side effects from the chemo. He only got nauseous one time, and that particular time was Christmas morning. The sickness was more to blame on being excited for Santa than drugs. There were only a handful of times that he had a fever that required a three-day hospital stay. As the end of the first year of chemo got close, we were getting excited. We had this! It wasn't so bad. Treatments after the first year would cut back to once a week and then drop down to once a month. We could hardly wait, it was so close. Just one week, and our first year of treatments would be behind us. And then there was a fever.

CHAPTER 14

The Infection

*   *   *

ETHAN WAS PRETTY GOOD AT diagnosing his own ailments. Every time he had a fever, he knew. And not only did he know he had a fever; he could also tell me if it was a "hospital fever" or just a "little fever" before I even checked. He was always right.

It was the morning of my birthday, and chemotherapy was done for the week. Blood counts were good, so we were heading home for the weekend. Our dog, Rosie, a basset hound, had just had her first litter of puppies. They were surprise puppies and a strange breed. The neighbors' Siberian husky came over for a visit when she was out for a potty break.

We were all ready to head out, and I plopped Ethan up on the counter to take his morning dose of pills.

"Mom, I had a fever last night."

"Did you?" I questioned and thought it was odd he didn't tell me last night.

"Yes, I did."

"Was it a bad hospital fever or just a little one?"

"It was a hospital one."

"Are you sure?" I was still surprised that he didn't mention it the night before.

"Yeah, I'm sure."

I took the thermometer out and checked his temperature. No fever now. "Are you sure you had a fever?" I asked him again.

"Yeah, I'm sure. Can we still go see puppies?" And there it was. He didn't tell me because he didn't want to miss out on puppies. At the same time, he knew he wasn't feeling well and should go to the hospital.

So we decided, instead of heading home now, we would stop by the clinic and get things checked out and get blood drawn just to be safe. Because he didn't have a fever now, I figured we would get the go ahead to go home. Mystery fevers were nothing new, and more often than not, they would come and go with no apparent reason. The high ones that stuck around for a few hours were the ones that landed us in the hospital. I didn't think this one was going to, but I didn't want to risk it, being so close to the end of our first year of treatment. I was convincing myself this was no big deal, but at the same time, my gut was telling me otherwise. This little boy who was so excited to meet some puppies would not have told me about this fever if he wasn't concerned about it himself. He didn't put up much of a fight at my suggestion to go get checked out either.

We arrived at the clinic and told them his claims of having a fever in the night. There was still no fever now, but we wanted to get checked out. Still no fever, but the pediatrician found one heck of an ear infection. There went our weekend! Three days in the hospital, here we come.

We headed up to our other home away from home to get comfortable for the weekend and wait for our antibiotics. After the antibiotics started, Ethan's fever returned, and it was a high one. Even after Tylenol was administered, it just kept on. Hovering between 102 and 103. We left Ethan with a string of grandmas on Saturday night so we could attend a wedding and returned on Sunday morning.

Upon our return, we found Ethan to be getting worse instead of better. Seemed like the ear infection was leaving, but the fever wasn't, and now he had pneumonia to deal with. Instead of going home Sunday like we expected, we had to camp out in the hospital for the rest of the week. Just a few more days in the hospital—we can do this, I was thinking to myself. It's only days away, and then our life will get much easier. Let's just get through this, and everything else will be smooth sailing. I was trying to stay positive and giving myself a pep talk, because who was I kidding? This totally sucked, and we were all so tired of it. Just as I convinced myself we could handle this, that's when Grandma Elsa came to visit. Again.

Ethan was lying in his hospital bed channel surfing, and he kept glancing out the door. The door was closed and had a small narrow window. Every time he looked out, I would naturally look that direction and wait for someone to come through the door. No one ever came in, and he just kept looking like he was expecting someone. I didn't even see anyone walk by.

After this went on for several minutes, Ethan said, "Mom, go get my grandma Elsa."

"What is she doing?"

"Go tell her to just come in here."

Ethan also had a Grandma Elsie, who was alive and well and sitting just to Ethan's left side in the corner of the room. I said, "Ethan, Grandma Elsie is sitting right here."

"No, Mom, not her—Grandma Elsa." And he emphasized the *a*, like I was so dumb as to think he didn't know the difference between his grandmas. "She's out in the hallway; just go get her."

"Ethan, Grandma Elsa is in heaven, remember?" He hadn't asked about her or talked about her in months.

"I know that, Mom, but now she's in the hallway. Tell her to just come in here."

Every hair on my body stood on end. The rational adult part of my brain tried to convince me that my kid was hallucinating because he'd had a 103-degree fever for days. The part of my brain that knew better sometimes than to listen to the adult told me that Grandma Elsa has been here before, and something terrible was about to unfold.

I walked over to the door with a gut-wrenching pain that made me want to vomit; I shook the whole seven steps from my chair to the doorknob. I pulled open the door with a chill running through my body, eyes clenched shut, knees trembling, and every hair on my body still on end. I was praying inside my head, "Please let my great-aunt be standing in the hallway, or some other lady with brilliant white hair standing outside this door." I swung the door wide open and stepped out into the hall. There was no one. A couple of nurses were chatting at the desk. "Look, Ethan, no one is out here."

"She was just there, Mom. Where did she go?" There was disgust in his voice as he said it.

A terrible feeling of dread took over my body. I could feel all the blood leaving my face, and my legs felt like they were going to collapse beneath me.

One of the nurses must have noticed the look about me because she asked if everything was okay.

"Just fine," I replied. "Was there anyone outside this door in the last few minutes?" I asked them. No, they hadn't seen anyone for a while. "Would you mind checking Ethan's temperature again?" No problem. I desperately wanted him to be hallucinating so this feeling would leave me, but I knew he'd seen her. Fever or not, I believed that she was out there.

The nurse ran the thermometer over his fore-head, looked at it surprised, and ran it over again. Then she grabbed the tympanic thermometer and checked through his ear. One-hundred-six-point what? Time to call the doc.

Ethan's pediatrician was the doctor on call that evening. It was decided that first thing in the morning, Ethan would be transferred to the University of Minnesota for further testing and treatment. His pneumonia wasn't responding to any of the antibiotics, and though it had only been a week, he should be showing some signs of improvement by now, even if just a little, and yet he continued to get worse. His chemo was on hold while an infection was on board, so it was best to get him to Minneapolis as soon as possible.

We left the hospital around eleven o'clock Monday morning by ambulance and headed to the airport. Once again, Grandma flew with Ethan so his dad and I could make arrangements with work and school and get some things packed. This time was different. This time we had no projected plans for discharge. No "about a month" to tell everyone. This time we had no idea what was going to happen. We just had to go. We told everyone in person this time around. "We're leaving, no idea how long; we'll keep you posted and hope to be back soon." And off we went.

Once we arrived in Minneapolis, I felt relieved. There were so many doctors waiting for us and ready to tackle the unknown. We were greeted by our regular oncologists, and they introduced us to some pulmonologists and infectious-disease doctors. Always new faces when the doctors were involved because it was a university hospital, so students were rotating all the time. They started Ethan on a stronger antibiotic and also threw an antiviral and antifungal into the mix. Those were the two things we really didn't want—viruses and fungi—because there was limited treatment for either of them, and his immune system was already weak. Ethan, as usual, adjusted well to the hospital—a little better than the rest of us.

Our first few days there were just a waiting game. Waiting around to see if these medications were going to work. No one was really sure what type of infection was invading his lungs, but it was a persistent one. They had some ideas of what it could be, but they weren't certain. At this point Ethan had a continuous flow of oxygen, and he was not impressed with having the cannula in his nose at all. His oxygen saturation hovered in the mideighties most of the time while the oxygen tube was just near his face. When we could actually get it directly in his nose, he would hit the high eighties at best. After the first few days with no improvements showing on his chest X-rays, they decided to do a bronchoscopy. The purpose of the procedure was to wash some of the junk out of his lungs and collect a sample of it to determine the exact type of infection he had.

The bronchoscopy was probably the most horrifying thing we had experienced since this whole ordeal started a year ago. He wasn't sedated because he had to be able to breathe and cough. Some kind of instrument was put into his windpipe while he was fully awake and the head of the bed was elevated for him to sit straight up. There were so many people holding him down and holding him still. I was not allowed to be in the room once they started, but I stayed right outside the door. The screams of pain and fear that came out of my three-year-old will haunt me for the rest of my life. It was a sound I will never forget. There was a gushing sound, with gagging, followed by screams of terror. It was a quick procedure, but it felt like hours from the other side of the closed door. When it was over, his breathing did ease up a lot, and they were able to collect adequate samples to find out exactly what had taken over his lungs. We waited some more.

The waiting game wasn't a very long one this time. We had a diagnosis by the end of the day: pneumocystis carinii pneumonia. A type of pneumonia that is not common in healthy people, it is an opportunistic infection that gets hold of people with a weakened immune system. It's a type of fungus that isn't easy to treat but is treatable. Great! We know what this is now, so we'll just hang out here until this junk goes away and we'll be home, however long it may take. He was already getting a couple of strong antifungal drugs, and by holding off on his chemotherapy, his own immunity should start to work in his favor.

Ethan remained stable and in about the same condition as he'd been in since we got there. With the exception of many nosebleeds from the oxygen in his nose, he was the same happy, contented kid. Because he was in good spirits and we had been there for over two weeks, with no possible discharge date in the near future, his dad and I let loose and let some other family members stay there with him while we went back home and worked here and there for a few days. We tried to take turns, but it didn't always work out that way, and often we were passing each other on the road or had only a night or two at home together with neither one of us at the hospital. The last year had almost put us in the poorhouse with cut work hours and unexpected hospital stays. The travel expenses and mounting hospital bills were overwhelming, and this extended visit to Minneapolis was not helping our situation at all. Ethan's dad tried to be home during the week because he had a Monday through Saturday job. I tried to go home on weekends because I was a bartender and the best tips came on the weekends.

On this particular week, I left Ethan on a Wednesday night and had plans to return on Sunday afternoon. I called several times a day while I was away, and things remained the same. I arrived back to the hospital early Sunday evening, a little later than planned. Just before I got there, things for Ethan started getting a little weird.

After I arrived, he was sitting a little sideways on his bed and was giggling because "I can't stay straight, Mom."

"You can't?"

He giggled some more. "Nope."

I giggled with him, thinking he was just being goofy.

My mom informed me that he'd been doing that for the last hour or so. She also thought he was just being goofy. He would tip sideways, sit like that for a bit, and then giggle and correct his posture. It wasn't until later in the evening when he went to the bathroom to get ready for bed that we realized this probably wasn't something funny anymore and something was wrong neurologically. He wasn't able to sit upright on the toilet without me holding him up straight. Something was definitely wrong.

We called the nurse in, and the pediatric resident on duty came in and did a thorough neuro exam with him. Everything seemed to check out normal except the fact that he couldn't sit up straight or stand straight without help. The resident ordered a CT scan first thing in the morning and put him on hourly checks throughout the night. Ethan slept great all night considering he was awakened every hour.

Sometime between his last neuro check and the CT scan, something went horribly wrong. When we woke Ethan up to get ready for his CT, he was unable to talk. His big-bright-sparkly blue eyes desperately wanted to say a million things, but nothing would come out. That was the first time in the whole year of everything terrible that happened to him that I could see real fear in his eyes. It was a "Mom, I'm so scared, help me" look, and he couldn't express it. And I couldn't help. It was beyond devastating. Not only was he unable to talk, but he seemed to have lost some movement in both of his hands and in one leg. His little body looked like an old man's that hadn't got out of bed for a year. And the fear on his face was real. They changed his orders from a CT scan to an MRI, and he was immediately taken to the lower level of the hospital for the testing. Another waiting game.

The MRI results came back and showed lesions on the basal ganglia. I had no idea what that meant, and everything they said just poured into my ears as nonsense. I understood nothing at all. There was no evidence of a stroke, and the lesions appeared to be similar to what a patient with multiple sclerosis has. There was a possibility that he was born with these lesions, but there was no previous MRI to compare it to. Whatever this was that he was experiencing was likely not permanent, as there was no sign of lasting damage in the MRI and he should improve over time. Every day, twice a day, someone from physical therapy and someone from occupational therapy would come and work with him to regain his movements and speech. It was a mystery. Whatever caused this or what it was remained unknown.

It was only a few days that seemed like forever before his voice came back. I had always wished for just five minutes of peace some days because he talked constantly, but never again after that day.

The hand movements came back just shortly before the talking, but the walking wasn't quite so easy. He was given a tiny little walker and made a few steps every day in his hospital room. I left to grab lunch one afternoon in the cafeteria and came back to find him all the way across the room. He was standing and painting a picture.

"Look what I made you, Mom!" he yelled with excitement. He was so proud, and so was I. It was a big blob of green and blue nothing, but it was great. I was so impressed that he walked all the way across the room. "It's a booger!" And he erupted with laughter.

Aside from this minor setback, Ethan seemed to be responding well to the antifungal medication, and we hung around for just a few more days; with another improved chest X-ray, we might just be able to bust out of this joint and continue the treatment as an outpatient at home. They were still waiting for some cultures in a lab somewhere in this hospital, but thinking this pneumonia was slowly but surely responding to treatments, things were looking up. All the white, cloudy junk that showed up on the X-rays was gradually disappearing. There were still obvious spots of pneumonia everywhere, but not anything like it was when we arrived. A month in the hospital was plenty, and we were ready to go home.

CHAPTER 15

Prognosis

* * *

IT WAS THE MIDDLE OF November, and we had been hanging out in the hospital for over a month. Ethan had a CT scan of his chest just to see how things were coming along, and we planned to head home at the end of the week. The doctors were confident that the infection was under control enough for him to continue the treatments at home. A CT scan just to make sure they weren't missing anything, and we would be on our way.

The day after the CT scan, we started the day with much excitement about the possibility of discharge. We didn't get any results from the scan the day before, so I thought no news was good news. After Ethan had his breakfast, I left him to get my own, take my morning walk around the campus, and head to the Ronald McDonald house for a shower. Breakfast, walk, shower. The same everyday routine. I stopped by the café to grab a coffee for myself and a Coke for Ethan before I headed back to his room. There was vegetable soup that looked so good, I couldn't pass it up. I opened the door to his room and said, "Hey, kid."

"They're looking for you, Mom. What's wrong?" All the while he did not look away from whatever was on TV.

"Maybe they're going to tell us we get to go home soon."

"No, something's wrong. They were calling you."

It's just amazing how a little person of only three years has it all figured out. Just as he finished his sentence, the overhead page came again.

"Jennifer Berreth, please report to unit 5B."

In that instant, my knees buckled, and my whole body trembled. I knew then something was wrong.

Ethan said, "See, Mom! Something is wrong; they're looking for you."

"They" don't go to so much trouble to find you when there is good news to be delivered. I walked to the bed-side table, completely out of breath from the fear of the unknown. I felt like I just ran up twenty flights of stairs without stopping for a breath. What could they possibly have to say, I wondered to myself. Things are going well. The hot soup and coffee were all over the cafeteria tray I was carrying them on because of my sudden trembling.

As I walked to the sink to wash the hot soup from my hands, the lead oncologist entered the room. "Oh, I'm glad you're back. Can we talk privately?"

They don't deliver good news privately as I have learned in the past, and they don't deliver the bad news in front of the kid, I also learned. I told Ethan I would be right back.

"What's wrong, Mom?"

"I'm not sure. You just watch TV, and call the nurse if you need to. I'll be right back."

"Okay, Mom." And he turned up the TV as I took the longest walk of my life.

It was only around the nurse's station and one left turn into the tiny little room where I was about to have my everything turned upside down. There was one doctor already sitting there, the one that accompanied me, and two more followed. My heart was beating so fast I could hear it and feel it through every inch of my body. It felt like a train was running through my head. Each one of them had that look about them. The sympathetic one. The one that says sorry before they actually say sorry.

I had to swallow my whole stomach. What are they going to say? Whatever it was, I knew it wasn't good. I closed my eyes for a moment and took a very deep breath to brace for the impact.

"Jennifer," the oncologist started, "this is doctor so-and-so, our lead pediatric pulmonologist, and this is doctor something, our lead infectious-disease doctor, and this is," and I stopped listening at that point A shrink maybe, in case I totally lost it. I could still hear and feel my heart pounding in my ears. "Shut up, shut up, shut up. Don't say anything. I want to go home. We want to go home. Shut up, shut up, shut up," is what I was screaming in my head.

And so she proceeded. "The infection that Ethan has, aspergillus, does not have a cure or treatment. What we do when a person has an aspergillus infection that doesn't respond to medication is remove the infected tissue."

"Oh good, so we can just cut this shit out?" I breathed a sigh of relief as I asked the question.

She shook her head no and said, "I'm sorry. Ethan's infection has covered all the lobes of his lungs, and only a small percent, less than five percent, of his lung tissue is not infected. So it is not possible to remove it. The treatment we are giving him has not decreased the infection at all, and there is nothing left to do."

"Can't he have a lung transplant?" I was grasping at straws. I would have given mine away right that second.

"That is a long process, and he won't live long enough."

"Why?" All I heard was, "Blah, blah, blah." "I'm so sorry" was all they kept saying. What now? My whole body was shaking.

"We will keep him as comfortable as possible. When his breathing becomes too difficult, we will administer morphine to help him relax. He will just stop breathing. He's been fighting this so long that his little body is just going to get tired and quit."

"What? When?"

"A week, maybe two. Now is the time to start making arrangements."

"*What?*"

"Someone will help you."

"What?"

"Can we call someone for you?"

"Oh my God, what?" I couldn't hear anything and just kept saying what over and over. I couldn't breathe. Everything was spinning.

"Should we call someone for you?" they asked again.

"What?" I need air! I need to get out of this tiny little room. "I just need some air. May I leave?"

"Can we call someone for you?" they asked yet again.

"Can someone please just go tell Ethan I had to go and I will be back soon?"

"Absolutely."

I didn't want to talk to him when I was crying, and even though I hadn't completely lost it yet, I was about to. "Tell him I went to get his dad."

I left the hospital. I couldn't get out of there fast enough. My eyes were burning from holding back my tears, and there was a lump in my throat that I couldn't swallow. I walked. I walked down the hundreds of steps to get to the river, away from all the people and all the bad that had just flooded my ears. I stood by the river and did nothing but stare. Not a single thought in my head. I just stared at the water and didn't move. I stood there long enough to lose the feeling in my fingertips and my toes. I walked back up all the stairs and the half block to my car behind the Ronald McDonald house, and I sat. An hour. Maybe two. Then the tears finally came. I cried.

My cries turned into uncontrollable sobbing, and then I screamed. Why? How does this stuff happen to a baby? He was just a baby. I thought of all the things he would never get to do. Go to school, go to the prom, drive, get a job, start a family. Nothing. It was all going to be over before he was even old enough to understand. Why? Then I sent up a prayer. Out loud as I sat in my car. I didn't pray to a God, like most people would, but I prayed out loud to my grandma. I knew she was out there somewhere and listening. She warned me before the cancer diagnosis, and she warned us about this. "I'm taking Ethan; you just never mind" is what she told me in my dream. "Please don't take my little boy" is what I begged her while I was sitting in the cold in my car all alone. "Whoever is up there listening to me, please don't take him."

I called my mom, still sobbing. "Please get here."

"Jen, what, oh my God, what?"

"They said he's going to die."

"What?"

"They said a week, maybe two. Please get here."

I hung up and dialed his dad. "You have to come back right now. He's not going to pull through this."

I made only those two very brief phone calls; I was worried about Ethan, having been alone for so long. I was gone for hours, and he was probably scared. I sat and cried for another ten minutes or so, and then an overwhelming sense of calm came over me. What is this? The calm before the storm. I had such a strange sense of relief. It was a very strange feeling. I was warm. I felt safe, like none of this day ever really happened at all. I stepped out of the car and headed back to the hospital. Headed to unit 5B to have yet another one of those horrible conversations that people should never have to have with their children. "You have cancer, and this is really going to suck" was a bad one. How would we have this conversation? "You beat the cancer, but…" I had no idea what I was going to say to him. How do you go about explaining death to someone who hasn't even lived yet?

"Where's my dad?" was the first thing he asked when I got to his room.

"He's coming." I was glad they told him what I asked them to. "Grandma and Grandpa are coming, and your dad, and then we're going home." I had decided we were going home. I didn't know how yet, but we were.

"To my apartment?"

"Maybe. Maybe not home to your apartment, but home to Bismarck." Home to the people that made it home.

I snuggled up in the bed with my little man and just held on to him tight. Holding back my tears, I put my lips on his little baldhead and just sat. Thinking of things to say to him. Soon his room would be filled with family and friends, and I wondered if I would ever have another moment like this. Later in the night, I mustered up the courage to bring up the idea of him not being here any-more. No mention of the words *death* or *dying*.

"Are you getting uncomfortable when you breathe?"

"Nope."

"Is it getting hard to breathe?"

"No."

"Are you sure?"

"I'm okay, Mom."

"You know, if it gets real hard to breathe, you just say so. They can put medicine in your IV to make it easier to breathe."

"I know, Mom. I'm okay." He was busy watching TV while we talked, but then he put his little hand on top of mine and smiled. He still had the sparkle in his big-blue eyes.

He didn't look that sick. I even questioned the doctors about the dying process and how he didn't seem to fit the stages of death. They assured me that children are much different than old people and my experience with death was quite different than that of a child. Ethan's oxygen saturation was still hanging around the mid- to high eighties most of the time, but he didn't seem to be struggling.

"You know, if Grandma Elsa comes to visit you again and she wants you to go with her, it's okay to go with her. She'll take good care of you while you wait for Mom to come."

"I know, Mom. Can I sit on her lap?"

"Yes, you can." And then he slept. I just held on, with tears streaming down my face until I too was sleeping.

Visitors started pouring in early the next day. Everyone in the family made their way to Minneapolis to say their good-byes. "Please leave your tears at the door," I asked everyone. I didn't want Ethan to get scared. "If you have to cry, you must leave the room" was my firm rule. Everyone did great, and he enjoyed all the extra company and attention. I'm sure he knew something was wrong, but he didn't ask.

"We would like to go home," I told his oncologist during her morning rounds.

"That's not possible. If you drive home, he will likely not make the trip unless by ambulance."

"So let's get an ambulance."

We spent the better part of the day calling every ambulance service in the Minneapolis area, and not a single one would take us home without a very large up-front payment. We were busy trying to scrape up money among us to pay for a ride home. We suggested to Ethan that he ask the Make-A-Wish Foundation to get him home, but that was the craziest idea he ever heard of. "I'm going to Disney World, not Bismarck! Why would I want an ambulance ride? Grandma lets me ride the ambulance all the time." Grandma is a paramedic, so ambulances were exciting, but not that exciting. According to my smart little three-year-old, wasting his wish on an ambulance ride was the dumbest idea ever.

By some crazy luck, an ambulance crew from Bismarck was transporting a patient to Rochester, and they offered to stop by and take Ethan home. Wonderful. Our time to leave was set for seven o'clock the next morning, and it was against medical advice. Doctors at the hospital didn't believe he would survive the long ride home.

We had made up our minds. I didn't understand what the big deal was. If they were certain he was to die soon, was there a difference where it took place—whether that was in this hospital bed or the back seat of my car? I couldn't understand. We wanted Ethan to spend his last days at home. If death was our destination, I didn't know why a location made any difference. As long as he was surrounded by loving family, it really made no difference to me where he was; I just didn't want to be here, and he didn't either. We were ready to go home.

I was encouraged to sign a do not resuscitate order before the trip. I did, with little hesitation. I got some arguments from some family members, but I wasn't about to make him suffer through the trauma of CPR when it wouldn't buy him much more time anyway. Signing that document made the whole situation seem very real. Why does someone have to sign a DNR order to take a toddler home? It just wasn't fair.

Ethan said good-bye to his favorite nurses the night before, and the morning we left. Some of them even made a special trip to the hospital on their day off just to say good-bye. Tears were shed by many. Our ambulance arrived just as planned at seven o'clock, and we were on our way home.

While the ambulance crew was busy switching out all the devices that had to ride home with us, Ethan put his little hand over mine and stroked it like he usually does. His big-blue eyes had a mischievous sparkle, and a little grin was on his face. He leaned in close to me and whispered, "Did they tell you I'm gonna die, Mom?"

I gave him a look of disbelief. Where had he heard this? I made it clear to everyone not to say the D word in his presence until I had some time to discuss it with him. Aside from the little bit I told him about going with Grandma Elsa, I hadn't mentioned anything about death or dying. I didn't even say the word since I made the two phone calls a couple of days before. There was no chance he heard that. I was in my car two blocks away. I just stared at him, still puzzled and waiting for the rest of his thoughts. I had learned in the last year that this little person took in so much more than we realized and he knew way more than we could imagine, but this was a big deal.

He whispered to me again, still holding my hand, "It's okay, Mom. You don't have to worry or be sad. I'm not going to die."

I said to him, "Everyone dies, Ethan, but only God knows when."

He grinned so big and shook his head no and said very confidently, "I'm not gonna."

The conversation ended as the paramedics started to wheel him out of the room. I walked beside the stretcher and held his hand until we reached the ambulance. They loaded him up, I jumped onto the seat next to him, and we were headed home.

Ethan's eyes were wide as we pulled off the ramp headed west. "Holy smokes, Mom—he drives too fast!" The medics were scared, I'm sure, and worried they might lose a little boy in their ambulance on the way home.

"We just have to hurry and get back to Bismarck," I told him. "Everyone is waiting for you to get home."

"Can I see Rosie?"

"Maybe. We have to stay at the hospital, but maybe she can come there to visit." We had gotten Rosie, our basset hound, as a puppy, just before his cancer diagnosis. Rosie had to live at Grandma's house because we were never home, and our plans to move into a house were deterred by chemotherapy. We were on our way to see her puppies the day this all started and never made it.

"Does she still have puppies?"

"Yes, she does."

"Can I see them?"

"We'll see." First thing on my to-do list when we got home was to get Rosie and her puppies to the hospital for a visit. I didn't last long on the road, maybe fifty miles, and then I drifted off to sleep. We stopped somewhere on the road, and I got in the front seat, as it was more comfortable. I was so exhausted. I didn't know it yet at the time, but Ethan's little brother was busy growing inside me, and it was almost impossible for me to stay awake at all hours of the day.

Before I knew it, we were in the ER entrance of Med Center One and on our way to the sixth floor. Fastest trip from Minneapolis ever. It wasn't even one o'clock yet when we got settled in. Ethan was right—he did drive too fast! But we made it home with no complications. I was so grateful we didn't need that DNR order.

There were happy faces waiting to greet us. Some of them were forced, as I could see some struggling to hold back their tears. A whole corner of the hospital floor was set up with a couch, a coffee machine, and lots of chairs. I guess they suspected Mr. Popularity was going to get a lot of visitors. He often got visits from people I didn't even know. "I'm so-and-so, and I met Ethan at the gas station." The guy who delivered the milk, the one who brought the Coke. Ethan made an impression on many people in his few short years. We settled in, and we waited. Waited for the horrible moment when the breathing became too difficult and morphine would be needed. Waited for the horrible moment for it to end. We waited.

The first thing I asked of the hospital staff was, "Can Rosie come to visit?"

"Yes, she can!" was their quick response. As long as she was up-to-date on shots, she could be there as much as he wanted her there.

Once we got the go-ahead for her to visit, Grandpa brought her, and she didn't come alone. There were also puppies! Not all the puppies could come along, because she had twelve, but there were a few. Rosie stayed to visit the entire evening, and Ethan had a great time.

The next day, we had visitors all day long. There was not a quiet moment. Ethan loved it, and this was pretty normal when we were in the hospital at home. Two ladies with the Make-A-Wish Foundation stopped to visit, and although Ethan wanted to go on vacation, we lightly persuaded him to have an early Christmas party. And so the planning began. Ethan was given sale ads and catalogs to shop and plan the most spectacular Christmas party of a lifetime. He planned it all on his own, from the tree decorations to the appetizers to the guest list. Unfortunately, his guest list was way too long, and the hospital didn't have enough room to accommodate all the guests he wanted to invite, so he had to downsize to a fourth of the number. Grandparents, aunts, uncles, and Mom and Dad were all who could fit.

He ordered up some race-car bedsheets for his hospital bed and picked out his own Christmas tree. Not one, but three Christmas trees. Decorations included NASCAR, Scooby-Doo, snowflakes, tinsel, and the craziest lights ever made. The lights flashed and blinked in more patterns than he could count. His Christmas menu included turkey and smashed taters, no gravy, and gingerbread men with Superman capes. He had a choir ordered to sing Christmas songs while he ate his smashed taters, and he got to pick out more toys than a kid could ever use. He also decided that everyone coming to his party needed a present. He very thoughtfully picked out gifts for everyone on his guest list. He was an excellent party planner. He had a wonderful time and got a few surprises. Santa stopped by and brought him everything he asked for plus more. A Power Wheels bobcat was his favorite, and he cruised around the play area and ran some of us over in the process.

What a wonderful Christmas we had. We were sad to see it end, knowing there probably wouldn't be another one for him, not even the real one this year that was only two weeks away.

CHAPTER 16

When Ethan Met an Angel

* * *

ANOTHER DAY CAME AND WENT, and another. Soon two weeks were behind us. Ethan seemed to be doing okay. Oxygen saturation was remaining the same, and he wasn't struggling to breathe any more than he had since the pneumonia and fungal infection started. So we waited. We continued with breathing treatments four times a day with a respiratory therapist. Antifungal medications were still dripping into his IV around the clock. Weeks had passed, and it was almost Christmas.

Having delayed his chemotherapy for months now, the oncologist was concerned about the cancer treatments. What was going on with this fungus? This was supposed to take his life in under two weeks. We certainly didn't need to start any chemo to make things worse, but why was he still here? Why did he seem to be doing okay when they'd doubted he'd even make the long ride home? He hadn't had a CT scan since the one he'd had just days before our dreadful news—the one that had revealed his out-of-control infection. Another CT scan was ordered to see what this monster was doing.

In the previous days, before the CT scan was ordered, Ethan stopped taking his breathing treatments. He absolutely refused to go with the respiratory therapist. "I'm not sitting in that dumb tent anymore."

I asked why.

"Because I don't have to. I'm not even sick anymore!"

We tried to do breathing treatments in his room with different medication, and he insisted he didn't need those either. More often than not, he would push his oxygen away during the day, telling us he hated it and didn't need it anyway. Because "I'm not sick."

One afternoon our ambulance crew stopped by to visit and see how Ethan was doing. It was a short visit, and while they were there, Ethan kept looking behind them. I, of course, looked behind them too to see what he was looking at. Nothing behind them but a sink and an empty hallway. They too glanced back a couple of times to see what he was looking at.

When they left, Ethan asked me, "What's that other lady's name?"

"Jodie," I said.

"No, not that lady, Mom—the other ambulance lady."

I was trying to remember the names of the staff on previous ambulance rides, but that had been so long ago. Ethan insisted that he wasn't talking about another ambulance ride or a different crew. He wanted to know the name of the lady who was with Jodie and Stuart. "That lady who rode home from Minnionapples with us."

"Jodie was the only lady with us."

"There was another ditch doctor lady in there, Mom; she was sitting right beside you." His voice was disgusted that I didn't know who he was talking about.

I asked him, "Was it Grandma Elsa?" as a chill ran through me.

"No, Mom, it wasn't Grandma Elsa; it was a medic lady."

"Okay," I agreed with him, and then I said, "Maybe we had a guardian angel with us to help watch over Stuart's crazy-fast driving?"

"She wasn't an angel, Mom. I saw an angel before."

"You did?"

"Yep. A big fat man."

"Oh really? Where did you see him?"

"In the hospital, in Minnionapples. He was there when you were sleeping in the green chair. He had a magic bone."

"What was he doing with a magic bone?" I asked.

"He put it on my chest and sucked all the bad germs out of my lungs." He pointed to his chest and said, "Right here he touched me, and all the germs went away."

"What?" I said, almost laughing at his crazy story, but yet again all my hair was standing on end. "What did he say?"

"Nothing. He just laughed a lot. It was really bright, like the lights on my Christmas tree. All my germs are gone now, so I'm not sick anymore."

The last CT scan in Minneapolis had revealed an infection that covered 97 percent of his lung tissue. The CT scan over a month later—and two weeks after he was supposed to be gone—showed us one clear healthy left lung and a right lung that was clear except for one small spot.

Our doctors were consulting with infectious-disease doctors and pulmonologists from the hospital in Minneapolis to figure out a plan of action. No one was really sure what to do at this point. Do we keep up the treatments? They were obviously working from a medical perspective. What else would have decreased the infection? From Ethan's perspective, a fat guy with a magic bone had visited him in the night and sucked all those germs out of his lungs. None of it seemed possible. Medication for months, and this monster infection just kept growing. Now it's almost gone? It was decided that he would remain in the hospital and keep up with the treatments. Another game of wait and see. Chemotherapy was to resume.

"This looks hopeful, but don't get your hopes up too high," I was told.

This was a miracle that we shouldn't believe in just yet.

Soon Christmas arrived. The Christmas Ethan wasn't supposed to live to see. We got a day pass from the hospital to go home for our real Christmas. As soon as his morning treatment was done, he was cut loose from his IV, and off we went for a day at Grandma's house. Food, fun, and presents! We had to be back to the hospital by seven o'clock for evening treatments, so the day was short, but it was the best Christmas ever.

Soon the New Year had come and gone, and we were still in the hospital with no change. We were finally released in the middle of January, just in time to plan a huge birthday celebration. Who would have thought turning four would be such a milestone celebration? We started chemotherapy again, and Ethan continued his daily anti-fungal treatments, which made for some very long days in the clinic. There was never a break. Seven days every week. We spent the weekend at the hospital for treatments when the clinic was closed.

Occasionally there were conversations between Ethan and me about the fat guy with the magic bone. He also mentioned him to others. The conversations were brief and without too many details. The guy was responsible for his germs being gone, and Ethan was certain of that. There were motions and noises to go with his explanation of how the germs left his body, and it wasn't from medicine. He was fascinated with the lights that were involved. The lights came off the end of that magic bone.

"He tickled my toes with it," Ethan would tell me. "He laughed really loud when he tickled my toes."

There was very much excitement in his voice and in his eyes every time the subject came up. He wanted to talk about it, but he said he wasn't supposed to. He often got a little miffed with us when we didn't know what he was talking about and would question him. Talk of the fat guy with the magic bone was just a part of everyday conversations.

One Sunday afternoon in the spring following the long hospital stay, Ethan was playing in the living room and chatting with his dad. He was telling his dad again about how all the germs in his lungs just were sucked right out because of that fat man with the magic bone. He was demonstrating with noises and movements. He rattled off all the colors.

His dad laughed in my direction and said, "Can you believe this kid? Where does he come up with this stuff?" A very good imagination was my best guess.

Ethan shot him a look of obvious disgust at the comment. He put Ethan in his lap to distract him from his story, which we had now heard more times than we could count.

Just a few moments after Ethan's dad distracted him from his story, I was headed out the door to go to my grandma's house. The cost of Ethan's medication was almost more than what his dad and I made together in a month, and someone left money with Grandma to help us out.

When I got in the car, I called her to let her know I was on my way. She wondered if Ethan was coming along. I had decided to leave him home because it was still hard for him to get around. His legs were weak, and we'd have to drag his wheelchair or walker with us. I wanted to make it a quick trip so I wasn't tired for work and school the next morning.

Grandma's response was, "That's too bad; I have a magic bone for Ethan to make a wish on."

I had completely forgotten that Ethan called the wishbone a magic bone. Every time Grandma cooked a turkey or chicken, they would break the magic bone to see who got to make a wish. I sat for just a second after Grandma said *magic bone*, and once again, every hair on my body was standing on end.

There was a long silence, and Grandma said, "Are you still there?"

"Oh my God. This fat guy that Ethan keeps talking about, I know who it is. I have to go back upstairs. I'll call you back in a little bit."

CHAPTER 17

A Team of Angels

∗   ∗   ∗

I RAN BACK TO MY apartment so fast I nearly fell up the stairs. I stood by the door for a few minutes just to catch my breath and try to seem calm. I went immediately into the closet to dig through old photos that had been packed away since before Ethan was born. Put away in my box of photos was a picture or two of my great-uncle. I was on a mission to find at least one.

Uncle Skeeter was my grandpa's brother on my mother's side of the family. He was a very large man, with an unforgettable boisterous laugh. When I was a kid, I spent many nights at the farm with Grandma and Grandpa with my cousins, and we would all pile up in the living room to sleep at night. Skeeter would show up every day around seven in the morning for a cup of coffee. He and Grandpa would talk about the weather and farming and whatever gossip was going around at the time. If we weren't out of bed by the time he was done with his first cup of coffee, he would stand at the bottom of the pullout couch, pull his pliers from his belt, and pinch every one of our toes and roar with laughter. The madder we got, the harder he'd pinch and the louder he'd laugh.

In my box of photos, I came across an album I'd made for Grandma Elsa when she turned ninety. I hadn't known the album was in the box, but it was perfect. I wanted Ethan to look through it. I placed the album on the coffee table in front of Ethan. I said, "Look at this book I made for Grandma Elsa. There are some pictures of you in there somewhere." He wasn't very interested in it, so I opened it to the first page.

"Who's that, Mom?" he asked.

I told him that was Grandpa's dad when he was younger.

He started looking at all the pictures, and I went and sat in the dining room and watched him as he paged through the photo album. One page after another, and he just glanced at the pictures before turning to the next page. Then his eyes widened, and he beamed with excitement and squealed, "See, Mom, you know him! That fat guy with the magic bone—he's right here! Right here he is, Mom!" And he flipped the book around to show me the picture.

He flipped it around to show his dad and went on with his story for the second time that day, this time with much more enthusiasm. "He touched my chest right here...and all the germs just got sucked out of my lungs."

With tears streaming down my face and Ethan telling his dad his magic-bone story again, I turned to grab the phone, to tell my mom what Ethan had just revealed to us. When she answered, I sat back in the chair and noticed that Ethan wasn't done yet. He was still paging through the album and found a couple of more people whom he knew.

I sat in the corner as my mom was saying, "What, Jen, what? You're scaring me here. What is going on?"

I told her to just hold on while I listened to Ethan tell his dad about the guy in the photo album, just as if he had seen him yesterday. "Do you remember this guy? He's that guy with Reggie the rock star, and he held on to me when I walked. Remember? He played basketball in my room." Reggie was Ethan's physical therapist, and he called him a rock star because he played in a band when he wasn't at the hospital. Ethan looked at me and said, "Remember when he helped me paint that booger for you, Mom?"

I couldn't believe what I was hearing. The person in the album who Ethan thought was a physical therapist in Minneapolis was actually my mom's cousin, Uncle Skeeter's son, who had passed away many years before I was born. I asked my mom if she could hear what Ethan was saying. I went and sat a little closer to him. He didn't need his walker anymore at Minnionapples because that basketball guy always helped him was what he was telling his dad as I sat on the phone and listened.

He continued flipping through the album. "Do you know this lady too, Mom? The paramedic lady?"

"Yes, I do know that lady, Ethan, but she's not a paramedic."

"Yes, she is, Mom."

"No, I'm afraid she's not."

"How come she was in the ambulance with us then?"

"She wasn't."

"Uh-huh. Mom, she was sitting right beside you. Remember, Stuart was driving fast, and she was sitting by you?"

The extra medic was Sharon, who was also gone. She had been with Grandma in my birthday dream over a year earlier.

All the little strange things he'd said and done over the last few months now made perfect sense. Ethan didn't have just one guardian angel; he had an entire team of them.

CHAPTER 18

The End of Infection

*   *   *

ETHAN'S FOURTH BIRTHDAY WAS THE most celebrated one to date. Being four years old was something special to celebrate. He wasn't supposed to make it to Christmas, and here we were two months later celebrating his birthday. We continued with clinic visits seven days a week, because no one was really sure yet what this infection was up to. It was still there, according to CT scans, but the small spot that remained was neither growing nor shrinking. Treatments continued to keep it from growing. We also had chemotherapy. There wasn't a big risk to his immunity in this phase of the chemo, so they figured as long as the antifungals stayed on board, he would remain safe. We were so tired. Ethan was tired, and I was tired.

Ethan's little brother was scheduled to arrive on July 12, and I wasn't looking forward at all to being more exhausted. Ethan was still struggling to walk in the summer. He didn't care for his walker much because, even after many adjustments, it made his back ache. I often had to carry him from the car to the third floor of the clinic, and that distance doubled on the weekends when we had to have treatments in the hospital. I dreaded having to carry a baby and him!

Aiden came to us ten days early, just the same as his big brother, except he came a couple of days before my scheduled induction. As with my previous pregnancy, I had developed preeclampsia. I was told over the holiday weekend to relax, kick my feet up, and check into the hospital on Monday morning to induce labor. Because I am bad at following directions, I went home and painted the living room. Ethan went home with my mom that evening so my roommate and I could tackle the painting project.

We took a short break and sat on the couch for a few minutes. When I stood up to continue painting, a strange noise followed me. It felt like my hip cracked, but it sounded real weird.

"Oh my God, that sounded wet," my cousin said from across the room.

"It did, didn't it?" I took a couple of steps and realized it *was* a wet sound and it wasn't my hip cracking. My water had just broken.

As my cousin and my roommate ran frantically around the house gathering my things, I was calling my mom to tell her to please come back—I was headed to the hospital. My favorite place.

I put on some fresh pants and headed to the car. Fresh pants were obviously a terrible idea. As soon as I opened the car door, baby boy number two moved a little, and a huge gush of fluid splashed onto the driveway, leaving me standing in the middle of a small lake.

I arrived at the hospital around eleven. I checked in, disrobed, and got comfortable while a couple of nurses started the IV and hooked up all the monitoring devices. I was dilated to six and hadn't felt a thing yet, except for the constant trickle of fluid. They decided to call the doctor right away and get some Pitocin on board while they waited for the doctor to arrive. I protested. I had done this before, and there would be no Pitocin anywhere near me until the doctor was here and waiting to catch my baby.

The doctor arrived, the Pitocin was started, and not a full twenty minutes later, I was holding my baby boy. This time around was so much easier than the first. He was perfect. Aiden Jensen, seven pounds eight ounces and twenty-two inches tall. Here comes another new normal.

I got a few days of freedom from clinic visits while I was in the hospital. Various family members and friends took turns toting Ethan back and forth for his infusions every day, but as soon as I broke free, the clinic routine was in full swing again.

Ethan was very determined to walk by himself so I wouldn't have to carry him and his baby brother. He was very worried about how hard I had to work. He did so well. Only a couple of times did he tire out, and I had to lift him and drag him down the hall with my one free arm. He had ditched his walker completely by this point, and I was grateful for that. One less thing to carry!

By the end of the summer, Ethan developed an allergy to one of the antifungal drugs, and it had to be discontinued. I can't say I was sad in the least bit. A tad worried but also relieved. Nothing had changed in the size of the infection in months, and not having that one drug on board cut our time in the clinic in half.

During the summer of 2003, the same summer after our big hospital stay and Aiden's birth, we had some interesting things going on. Ethan started behaving oddly, and I couldn't put a finger on exactly what was happening to him. Also during this summer, just two weeks after Aiden was born, Grandma Agnes fell and broke her hip. She was taken in to surgery for a repair and didn't wake up. The doctors thought it was a blood clot. She went peacefully in her sleep. She was ninety-two. We were devastated!

Traveling back and forth from home to the funeral, some more interesting things about angels and the great beyond emerged from my little man. He informed my mom that, while he was real sick and the fat man came to visit, his mom was supposed to pick out a stone and put his name on it. Grandma Elsa and the fat man told God that he wasn't going to get a stone yet and that God had to wait. There was a star for him in the sky. "God already had the star ready for me, but Grandma and the fat man told him no, so he had to put that star in my eyes. That's why my eyes sparkle more now, because God put stars in them."

During the burial ceremony for Grandma Agnes, Ethan headed straight to Grandma Elsa's grave site. Though he had not been there before, he knew exactly where to find Grandma Elsa. He informed me that I was supposed to get him a stone like this and I was going to put it right there. He pointed to a spot near the rest of my family, which was a likely place I would have laid him to rest. "You didn't have to get me a stone and put my name on it though, because Grandma Elsa and the fat man said no." Once again, every hair on my body stood on end.

I felt relieved somewhat and thought about that spot on his lung. It was nothing. I knew it was nothing. Ethan was completely fine.

CHAPTER 19

Seizures–The Beginning

* * *

ETHAN'S UNUSUAL BEHAVIORS STARTED IN the summer of 2003. He had been a kid who loved his sleep since the day he was born, but he started waking up frequently during the night. He was quiet about it. I wouldn't have noticed at all had he not left behind evidence I would find the next day—little things like leaving the TV on or leaving the milk on the counter and an empty bowl on the coffee table from making himself a bowl of cereal. I'd often find him in the mornings in odd places, like in the tight corner between the wall and the couch or even on the steps. I questioned him about it. Was he in pain; did he not feel well; was he having bad dreams? Nope, none of that.

"I just wake up," he would say.

We tried having a warm glass of milk before bed and then moved on to things like melatonin and even Benadryl. Nothing helped. He started to look sick again. Big dark circles were under his eyes, and he had a general look of exhaustion. I knew something was wrong, but everything checked out medically. Blood counts were good, and the infection was the same. Everything was fine. Except it wasn't, and we just couldn't figure it out.

By the end of the summer, he started leaving the house in the middle of the night and wandering around outside in the dark. The first time it happened, I believe I aged twenty years in five minutes. I woke up in the morning to find the back door wide open. There was no sign of Ethan anywhere. I looked everywhere! Under every single bed, in every closet, all the cupboards, the basement, the garage, the car. Nothing. And just as I was about to call the police, I found him sleeping safely in his grandma's bed next door. Why she didn't find it necessary to tell me he was there the second he walked in is beyond my comprehension, but it became a habit.

I finally had to put a dead bolt on the top of my back door just to prevent his nighttime adventures and to keep my sanity intact. This new sleeping pattern carried on for a whole year, into and throughout his first year of school.

CHAPTER 20

Going to School

* * *

ETHAN STARTED SCHOOL IN THE fall of 2004. He was ready and so very excited. School didn't turn out to be the great experience we hoped it would be. There was such a remarkable change in my happy, bubbly, normal little boy, and we just didn't know what the problem was. The year of sleepless nights was a huge problem, but something more was going on—we just didn't know what. He wasn't able to keep up with the rest of his class academically. It seemed that everything he already knew and learned was just gone, and nothing new would go in.

Before he started school, he recognized all the letters of the alphabet, could count to one hundred with ease, could spell and sound out small words, and could also name all 206 bones in the human body. "A little ahead of the game," I thought. Once school began, it was all gone. He struggled to even write his own name and couldn't color a picture even close to inside the lines. He was frustrated, to say the least, and with his frustration came angry outbursts.

Angry outbursts every day in school became his normal by the end of the school year. Something had changed. Something was wrong.

Throughout the school year, Ethan missed almost every Monday for his routine blood draws and clinic appointment. He was still taking antifungal medication, but just an oral form. The chemotherapy would be over by the time the school year was done, and it was still a question as to what to do with the spot that remained on his lung.

Sometime during the spring, we toted Ethan to the University of Minnesota. He needed surgery to remove his port and to remove whatever spot was remaining from his massive life-threatening infection. It was still undetermined if the spot was infection that remained or just scar tissue from the infection. He hadn't been without antifungal drugs since the infection was found. We needed it out so if it was infection, it would not return.

When we arrived at the preop appointment before the surgery, there was much surprise and excitement from everyone. The surprise and excitement came from seeing Ethan alive and well more than a year after they'd sent him off with a death sentence. The infectious-disease doctor was confident that the remaining spot on his lung was just an empty pocket surrounded by scar tissue, but it was best to get rid of it just for safety. It could be biopsied, but that was an invasive procedure just like the surgery to remove it. If infection was found in the biopsy, it would have to be removed anyway. So we would remove it in one surgery and be done with it regardless of what it was.

During our appointment with the infectious-disease doctor, the resident who was working with him commented that she had been reviewing Ethan's case and couldn't believe he was sitting here in front of us. She asked us if we had any religious affiliation. I informed her that we were Lutheran, but we didn't practice. Ethan had been to church only a handful of times in his life. He had missed out on Sunday school up to this point because he couldn't be around large groups of people with his compromised immune system. After he was able, we wanted to really live before we had to start an actual normal life again, and that didn't include an every Sunday, get-out-of-bed-early-when-you-don't-have-to church schedule. When I told her we did not practice our religion faithfully, she went on to say there really was no medical explanation for his recovery at all. No, there wasn't. We knew. His recovery, according to him, came from a fat guy with a magic bone that was lit like his Christmas tree. He visited in the night when no one else was looking, he laughed a lot, and he touched Ethan's chest with his magic bone and sucked all those icky germs right out.

The surgery didn't last long, just a few hours. We spent a few days in the hospital with a chest tube in place to drain the excess fluid. Ethan was in a lot of pain but in good spirits. He was excited to be free of his tubies. I was excited for freedom from all of it. We were discharged from the hospital within a week and went home with a bottle of morphine and a lot of scars. The scars were both mental and physical. We planned on having a party in a few months when school was out to celebrate the freedom— the throwing away of every single pill in our house. We were almost free. Free of treatments, free of infections, free of pills, free of breathing treatments, and free of sickness. We were almost free!

CHAPTER 21

Seizures—Continued

* * *

THE SLEEPLESS NIGHTS THAT HAD carried on for over a year continued. Several angry outbursts during the day continued. We made it through the school year, made it through surgery, and chemo was all done. That's when I started to see the seizures. I didn't actually see a seizure, but I saw the results of them. The things that were "off" that made no sense.

Because Ethan had missed so much school that year, it was decided that he would repeat kindergarten. Shortly before school ended, I noticed the result of the first seizure. Ethan was lying on the ground flat on his back for seemingly no reason at all. He would ride his bike in the yard or tootle around on his Power Wheels most days after school. I would occasionally glance at him out the window to make sure he was still there and safe. As soon as I would look away, a sudden movement would catch in my peripheral vision, and he would be lying in the grass or the dirt or whatever surface he was driving on. He would get up quickly, get back on his equipment, and continue what he was doing.

Every morning, Aiden and I had a routine where we would walk to the post office and stop at the grocery store. I would pull him in the wagon. Once school let out for the summer, Ethan would join us on our morning walk. Every day, almost like clockwork, we wouldn't make it to the end of the alley before Ethan was lying in the dirt. "How did you fall out of the wagon?" I'd ask.

"I don't know" was always his response.

I started walking backward to see if I could catch him in the act of jumping out, because it seemed like that's what he was doing—jumping right out. It was almost impossible for him to fall out and land the way he always landed, so I was sure he was just being goofy. I walked backward, and nothing happened. Mystery solved. So I quit walking backward. No sooner than I quit, he was in the dirt again. "Did you do that on purpose?"

"*No!*"

"Are you sure?"

"*No!*"

He was mad I had asked. If he wasn't doing it on purpose, what was going on, and why couldn't I catch him? It was more than a month into the summer before I finally saw what was going on, and I suspected it was some kind of neurological malfunctioning. I didn't call it a seizure, because like most people who aren't familiar with different kinds of seizures, I thought a seizure involved every part of the body twitching and shaking, lasted a long time, and was very dangerous. Whatever he had going on was a very fast twitch. It lasted only seconds but was very violent. It involved only the top half of his body, one arm and his head mostly. Sometimes both arms. It looked like someone invisible came up behind him and pushed the back of his head really hard, and the arms followed as if to catch his fall. Most of the time it was so quick he did catch himself before hitting the ground. Sometimes he didn't.

I mentioned his electrical malfunction to his doctors a few times, and because I hadn't seen anything other than him lying in the dirt up to that point, they decided the falling was from his gimpy leg and recommended more physical therapy. It didn't sit right with me, because falling out of a wagon didn't have much to do with a gimpy leg, but I agreed to more therapy. It wasn't going to hurt him, but I insisted that something was wrong and it was a neurological problem.

Once I witnessed it and was able to describe it better, he was put on an anticonvulsant. We made an appointment with a neurologist in Minneapolis. Ethan was scheduled for a hospital stay for three days to video monitor while he was hooked to an EEG. Three days passed and nothing.

Stubborn should have been his middle name. We headed home with no new orders. They concluded that whatever type of seizure he was having, this anticonvulsant was working, so we'd stick with it. I think the doctors thought I was completely nuts. I felt very defeated. I knew something was wrong in his brain, and I just couldn't catch it in the right moments for anyone else to see. He started falling down more, and when he was in a relaxed state, watching TV, just before sleep, or when I read him a book, there was continuous twitching of his upper body. The twitches didn't last long, but they came often, and it was disturbing. When he was upright and not sitting, he would slam into the ground.

The twitching just continued to get worse and worse. I couldn't get anyone to hear what I was saying, because I was the only one who ever witnessed the events. There was finally a day that I had a light-bulb moment. Ethan sat on the couch, just about to doze off, and the twitching started in full force. One twitch after another, after another and another. His upper body would jerk, and he wouldn't get more than a couple of seconds of relief, and he would do it again.

I don't know why I hadn't thought of it sooner, but I picked up the video recorder and started filming. I had had enough of no one listening to me, and now they were finally going to see what I saw. I knew this wasn't normal, but no one would believe me because they didn't see it. It seemed like with every twitch, a little bit more of my little boy and his bubbly, sparkly personality would disappear. A little bit of him was gone with every jerk, and there was nothing I could do to save him.

I captured ten solid minutes of almost continuous twitching on a video. I packed a bag, dropped off my tiny boy with his grandma next door, and drove Ethan straight to Minneapolis so I could say, "See! Look at this! Listen to me, dammit! This is not his leg causing this!"

My mom went with me to Minneapolis, and we were able to meet with a neurologist in the clinic the next day. I showed him the videotape I had made the day before, and my mom was able to induce a seizure by holding Ethan in her lap and telling him a story. The seizures weren't as bad as what he'd had the previous day, but they were still pretty obvious. It was obviously not his leg and not a problem more physical therapy was going to fix. His legs were completely relaxed and dangling in front of him. The legs didn't move a bit when his electrical malfunction occurred.

After the neurologist witnessed Ethan's short episode and watched the video a couple of times, he had an idea of what type of seizures Ethan might be having. He prescribed a couple of new medications and told us to discontinue what he was currently taking. An appointment was set up for him to have another video EEG in a week for three to five days so they could determine exactly what type of seizures these were.

We were feeling very defeated. Just when we thought all the yuk was behind us, we got a bunch more. We had celebrated and thrown away baskets full of pills. Now we just got more pills to fill up the baskets again. Ethan's new meds seemed to be helping, though. I didn't notice as many twitches from him, but he was still very restless at night.

We got ready for our next trip to Minneapolis, hoping to figure out the exact kind of seizure and get the right meds to take care of them. I was very hopeful that these awful things were only temporary and he would grow out of them. We were told that these are common in kids who have had leukemia, and they often go away in or before their teen years.

We arrived in Minneapolis and got settled into our room. Ethan was very impressed with the big TV in the corner, but he wasn't impressed to learn that the only thing that TV was doing was watching him. He couldn't watch it. Well, he could, but the only show it played was him. The next thing that didn't impress him was the attachment of the wires. It took a lot of creativity and a lot of threats for him to allow those things again. He screamed and protested the entire time. Three very long, very boring days were to come. Day one passed with not a single seizure or even a twitch. Day two had the same results. Day three and still nothing, so the wires were removed, and we were given our walking papers.

The removal of the wires proved to be twice as fun as getting them put on. We were just going to live in the hospital forever, or until the wires grew off his head enough for me to cut his hair underneath. "I'll be bald. I don't care! I was before." There were no changes in medications, as these seemed to be working. We'd revisit this if anything more came up.

We no sooner had put our toes on the pavement in the parking garage when *boom!* Down he went. "Are you okay?" I shouted from my side of the car.

"Yep."

I told him I was convinced that his stubborn little voluntary self had convinced his involuntary self to be a stubborn little brat too. He just giggled.

CHAPTER 22

More Seizures—Just Our Way of Life

✳   ✳   ✳

ONCE THE SEIZURES STARTED, WE never had a day with-out them. They just became a part of our life. We went through many medications and different combinations of medications. The meds would help for just a short time, never completely eliminating the seizures but decreasing them. Then we would be right back to where we'd started. It seemed like after each new medication or change in dos-age, they would get a little worse. We had regular EEGs and MRIs with med changes, and nothing ever worked.

Attending school with a seizure disorder proved to be disastrous for all of us. Every day was a challenge. Lack of sleep made it almost impossible for Ethan, and some-times me, to get out of bed. It was hard for Aiden too once he started school. Once we got to school, usually late, he would fight and often get sent home or sent somewhere to take a nap.

By the time Ethan was ten, seizures had complete con-trol of our lives. Eating, sleeping, going to work, going to school, even bathing were chores. He had to be belted to his chair at mealtimes so he wouldn't smash his face on the table or in his plate. He could eat through his seizures and carry on a complete conversation. He would check out for a second and then just continue right where he'd left off when it was over. They lasted just seconds, but there were so many. He had to start wearing a helmet anytime he stepped off the carpet to save his face and his teeth and to save his face from his teeth. Increases in medication became toxic in his body, and he would sleep for days on end. There were dizziness, vomiting, and sleeping. So what was better? Meds or seizures? We usually opted for more seizures—at least he was coherent and could function somewhat normally between the twitching. Broken bones and a beat-up face were just part of our everyday normal.

Ethan adapted well to every little change and was good at his situation. I tried, but every twitch sent my blood pressure up another point and added an inch to my waistline. I was stressed out. I was no longer able to work full time because the seizures scared off every babysitter who came through the door. I had a few good ones, and they would stick around just long enough to see him hit his face on something really hard, and then they would never return. The seizures were just everyday life to us, but to others, they were shocking. It was very disturbing to watch a small boy hit something that hard and just continue about his business like nothing had happened at all. When he complained that something actually did hurt, we knew it hurt! Almost every bone was fractured in one of his feet, and he never once complained about it hurting. We didn't even know there was a problem sometimes until it hurt bad enough to get it checked, and then we'd find other broken bones that were in different stages of the healing process.

Just before Ethan turned twelve and just after we had visited every neurologist in our area, we found a doctor who had some options for us other than medications. At this point, Ethan was running out of meds, I was running out of sanity, and we were open to anything. One option was to try a ketogenic diet. With his stubbornness and love of everything carbs, that option wasn't the best fit. Another option was a corpus callosotomy.

This was a surgery that involved cutting his brain in half to sever the connections from one side of the brain to the other. The surgery came with many risks, the worst being bleeding and death. We thought that would be the best option for him, but we needed time to discuss it and process the thought. This surgery seemed to be his best hope, ending with a 50 to 90 percent reduction in seizure activity if it was successful, but the risks were great. We spent a week in the hospital again hooked up to a video EEG and had many tests to determine if he was in fact a good candidate for surgery. He was. We just had to decide.

A couple of months of talks you should never have to have with your child took place. We discussed it in great detail many times. Hypothetical "What if this happens?" discussions. I was scared to death, but he was ready.

"You know you could die, right? You know what that means, right?"

"Yes, I know, Mom, but I'll be just fine. I'm sick and tired of these damn, dumb seizures, and they need to be gone! I'm tired!"

"So am I, bud, so am I."

"Just watch and learn," he told me. "I'll be just fine."

"Watch and learn" is what he always told me, and watch and learn is what I always did, and he never ceased to amaze me. And so it was a done deal. He wanted the surgery, knowing what the consequences might be, and we scheduled our appointment with the neurosurgeon.

We met the neurosurgeon at the clinic, and he went over in detail what he would do during the surgery, how long it would take, and what we could expect afterward. It didn't sound like a good time at all. Two months of recovery time. Having to learn things all over again like walking, talking, and eating. It would all come back if there were no complications, but the brain would need a great deal of time to do things on each side individually, without communication from the other side. When we do things like walk, we don't need to think about it. The left side just tells the right side that we're walking, and one leg follows the other. Ethan would have to tell the other leg to move, and it would take a couple of months to learn how to do this repeated commanding. He didn't care. He wanted it done.

Our surgery date was set for April 28, 2011. The surgeon was excited to help Ethan and loved his enthusiasm. Given the severity of Ethan's seizures, the surgeon guessed that he wouldn't be seizure free, but he was hoping for at least an 80 percent reduction and to get rid of the helmet and constant injuries.

Ethan was counting down the days for surgery. It was both scary and exciting. He was busy collecting little angel trinkets to take with him for extra backup protection. He informed me that his angels would be there with him and that he would be just fine. He said I didn't need to worry so much about it and could just watch and learn. I had put in my notice at work in preparation for his long recovery time. The neurosurgeon explained that after the surgery, Ethan would likely have to transfer to a rehabilitation facility, in a different state so I didn't expect to be able to work for several months.

CHAPTER 23

Brain Surgery

*   *   *

WE ARRIVED AT THE HOSPITAL in the morning the day of the surgery. Normal surgery stuff: nothing to eat or drink eight hours prior and arrive two hours early. The surgery was scheduled to start at eleven. Nothing ever goes as planned in a hospital, so we waited around in a tiny little room until noon. Next thing we knew, it was one o'clock. Ethan's lack of food and beverage since the previous night was making him a little cranky. Not long after one, a nurse came in and informed us that the doctor's previous surgery had experienced some unexpected complications, and it was unknown when Ethan would be taken in for surgery. We were still waiting at six o'clock. By eight o'clock that evening, we were still waiting, and his crabbiness was almost unbearable. "Can I just get some damn hot chocolate around here?" he would ask the nurse every time she walked by. "Why can't I just have some hot chocolate? I won't barf it up. I'm serious; I won't!" The doctor had finished his prior surgery a few hours ago but needed some downtime to eat and rest before he could begin with Ethan.

I was more than a little anxious already, and the fact that he had been working on someone else's brain for that many hours and was about to cut open my kid's head made me very uneasy. "Should the doctor maybe go home and sleep and do this tomorrow?" I asked. They assured me that he took breaks during the surgery and ate and rested throughout the day. This was how they did it, and everything would be fine. This was my kid's brain, and I was cooking up all kinds of scenarios in my head of the surgeon passing out with the scalpel from low blood sugar or taking a nap while standing up in the middle of the surgery. We were finally told Ethan would go to the operating room around nine.

I don't recall the exact time the surgeon finally arrived, but he came with the anesthesiologist and introduced him to Ethan and me. He told Ethan how they would put him to sleep and they would have to shave a lot of his hair off to cut the skull. Ethan listened and agreed. Once the surgeon was done, he would put Ethan's skull back and secure it with metal Band-Aids. Ethan was pretty excited about that part. He thought he could be like a superhero with metal plates in his head. They told him about the room he would be in when he woke up and that he would have a tube in his head when he woke up for the blood to drain for a couple of days.

"Can I get some hot chocolate around here when I wake up?"

They all laughed, and the doctor said, "Absolutely; you can have whatever you like when you wake up." He told Ethan then that he might have some trouble eating and drinking for a while, but the nurse or I could help him drink hot chocolate.

"Okay."

As soon as the operating room was ready, we were off. I was able to go in with him until he was sleeping. The nurse tried to take all the things he had collected from the bed, but he was having nothing to do with it. He said he needed those to help his angels protect him. He was serious enough that she thought she might lose an arm if she touched them, so on the bed they stayed.

When we got back to the operating room, I was finally at ease with what was about to happen and what could happen, but that was when the reality set in for Ethan.

He was scared. "Mom, I don't want to do this anymore; let's go home."

We had to have a few minutes to talk it out; this decision of ours was a good one. "What happened to watch and learn?" I asked him. "You got this!"

He grabbed hold of the blue velvet bag that was holding his angel collection. He looked at me and said, "I do." He took a deep breath and lay down. He tucked all the things back under his pillow, and tears were streaming down his cheeks. He was trying so hard to hold it together, and he made it really hard for me to hold it together. It took everything I had in me not to lose my cool and grab him off the bed and run.

As soon as the gas mask came into sight, he started screaming in fear. I started sobbing. As many surgeries and scary moments as we'd encountered in the past decade, this one was the worst. This was the one we had picked, and it was going to change our lives forever, whether it was for better or worse. Things were going to be different whatever the outcome was. Ethan knew it just as well as I did. He was squeezing my hand so hard, and we both cried. Through my sobbing, I told him to just breathe and promised I would be right there next to him when he woke up. Within seconds his crying stopped, and the only noise left in the room was the sound of my sobbing.

Soon all the machines were rushed to his bedside, and I was rushed out of the room by a tall masked lady.

CHAPTER 24

Waiting

* * *

THE WAIT WAS HORRIBLE. I sat and I paced, and I paced and I sat. The only things to break up the uncomfortable everything were the occasional phone calls I would get from family and friends who wanted to know how things were going. I cried a lot and thought too much: What if this was a bad idea? What if his seizures weren't any better? What if he bleeds? What if he never wakes up? What if the doctor cuts something he's not supposed to? Hours went by with no updates. What if something is wrong?

Finally, someone came out and approached me. "Are you Ethan's mom?"

"Yes."

"Jennifer?"

"Yes."

The two seconds it took for her to introduce herself and smile seemed like a lifetime. Everything in me was screaming for her to say something good. "Everything is going smooth in there. The surgery is about halfway over, and things are well." A huge sigh of relief.

I got a couple of more updates throughout the night. The best one was the last update. "The surgery is complete, and everything went well. The doctor is just going to take a short break to rest and then continue with stitching. He will come and speak to you when Ethan is taken to the recovery room and show you there."

It was well into the morning hours when the doctor finally came out. He told me that things were great in there. He'd had a little bit of complication getting the brain separated toward the end and had to "work the left side of the brain a little bit, so we may see some heavy bruising in the eyes," but he was very pleased with the operation. Because he didn't want us to be alarmed, he warned that Ethan might look very beat-up and strange. No affect, a blank stare, and no communication should be expected for at least the first week, probably two. After that, we would see where he was at with eating and walking and using his limbs. There would need to be extensive occupational and physical therapy to get him functioning as he had before the surgery. There were options for rehab facilities that we would discuss later, if or when it was necessary. We would take it one day at a time.

Off to the recovery room to wait some more, this time just for him to wake up.

A nurse led me through a short hallway and many doors. She warned me of the drain that was attached to a tube on top of his head and said I should expect him to wake up soon but not to say or do much. She wanted me to be prepared and repeated what the doctor had just told me on my way to her. I got up next to his bed and took in all the tubes and hoses running out of his body. The nurse grabbed me a chair, and I sat next to his bed, grabbed his hand, and laid my head near his to wait for some movement. All the little trinkets he'd taken to surgery with him were still there. Stuffed under the pillow, under his hand, above his head.

I didn't have to wait long for him to start moving a little.

He opened his eyes, looked at me, grinned a little, looked around the whole room, and spotted the nurse walking toward the bed from across the room. He didn't know or care that it was a completely different nurse than the one he'd had before surgery. He fixed his gaze on her, and it was an angry one. As soon as she was in earshot, he said to her through gritted teeth, "Where is my damn hot chocolate?"

I laughed out loud and said, "Oh my God, really?"

The nurse was a little confused—confused about the hot chocolate and confused that he'd talked the moment he opened his eyes.

I told her he had been waiting for hot chocolate since one o'clock the day before and that the other nurse had promised him a cup as soon as he woke up. If he could please have one, that would be really nice. "I am so tired and sure don't want to listen to him gripe about it anymore." I was laughing but was completely serious at the same time. The sound of his voice was music to my ears, but having to hear about hot chocolate for one more second would have been complete torture.

She had to check with the doctor. They hadn't been expecting him to wake up and immediately make food and drink demands, so there weren't even any diet orders yet.

Within minutes, the surgeon was standing at Ethan's bedside. "Did he just ask for hot chocolate?" The doctor directed his question at me.

Ethan looked right at him and said, "Yes, I want some damn hot chocolate. You said I could have some when I woke up, and now I'm awake. Isn't my surgery done? I want some hot chocolate."

The surgeon was a little more than surprised that Ethan was up and talking and asking for anything. He did a short exam, checked him over, and smiled the whole time he did it. He apologized for telling me what to expect, but this wasn't expected. "This is very good." He turned and told the nurse to get this young man some hot chocolate.

We moved into a private room on unit 5B. On our way down the hall, we noticed that the picture Ethan had colored with his aunt was still decorating the entrance of room 535. It had been hanging there for ten years. Once we got settled into our room, we had some more hot chocolate, and Ethan decided he wanted to sleep. I was so excited for his request to sleep because I hadn't been to bed in two whole days. He rested for the rest of the day and slept the whole night. It felt amazing.

The next morning he was hungry and asked for a bowl of cereal. When the cereal arrived, he got himself to the side of the bed with little help. He adjusted the bed table in front of himself and grabbed his spoon. He scooped up the cereal as we watched him in disbelief. He started lifting the spoon to his mouth with his right hand. The left hand followed right behind it. The right hand missed the mouth by an inch or so and the cereal landed on his shoulder, while the left hand popped him square in the left eye. After he was done giggling, he went after another bite. We teased him and told him to put it in his mouth, not on the bed, and he giggled some more.

He put some thought into the next few bites, and each one after the first went somewhere on his face, with most of it in his mouth. It was perfect after the fourth bite. He had the left hand tamed to sit nicely on his lap while the right hand headed for his mouth.

He spent most of the next two days sleeping off and on. He watched TV and played a few video games and seemed to have no trouble at all using the game remote. On day three they were able to remove the drain from his incision, and because he was free from that, he wanted to get the heck out of there. "Can we go home now?"

When the doctor came in to visit, he couldn't believe Ethan's progress. The doctor said, "What needs to happen for you to go home is you have to work with PT and OT to make sure you're safe and can do things on your own, so you have to walk." He had been up to the bathroom plenty of times but hadn't actually taken any steps. He'd just stood and turned around from the bed to the wheelchair and from the wheelchair to the toilet and back. "If you can walk for PT and they say you can go home, we will get you out of here by the weekend."

PT and OT both came at separate times that afternoon. He was given the green light by OT, but PT wanted him to take many steps and be able to use a walker before he could leave. Whether it was stubbornness or fear, he refused to take a step in front of anyone.

The couple of times I left him, I came back to find him in the bathroom or in the chair across the room. "How did you get there?"

I got a look like "Wow, are you dumb?" and he would say, "I walked."

"Why don't you walk with the physical therapist?"

"I can't."

"Why?"

"I don't feel like it."

IVs were removed, and not one single thing was keeping us there other than his unwillingness to walk in front of others.

On day four we made laps in the wheelchair around the campus, ate all our meals in the cafeteria, and didn't spend much time in our room at all. We ran into old friends in the cafeteria, and he had a few visitors while he was there. On Saturday, we had to be transported by ambulance to the new children's hospital. I do believe he was holding out on walking so he could spend a night or two in the new place and ride in an ambulance.

Once we settled into our room in the new place, he was using his walker back and forth to the bathroom in front of me. There was no PT person on duty on the weekend, just someone on call, so we were stuck for the weekend. By chance, someone in PT was there on Sunday and was willing to work with him that afternoon.

We were discharged from the hospital early Monday morning. One whole week in the hospital. One week. What was supposed to be *months* ended in a *week*.

He had a few small twitches on day three, and he was put on a smaller dose of the meds he was previously on. His discharge orders told us of things to watch for, what was normal, and what things to be concerned about. We were to expect bad headaches for a while, since everything was healing. We were to follow up with his neurologist in two weeks, have a follow-up appointment with the neurosurgeon in six weeks, and have the stitches removed in eight weeks. I could take them out myself, but if I wasn't comfortable with that, I could take Ethan to any health-care provider to have them removed.

I was very relieved and excited but also scared. How did he recover this fast? What do we do now? I didn't even have any work to go to for the time being, because he was supposed to be recovering in a hospital for months.

On the way home, he chatted all the way. He was reading road signs and asking what this one meant and that one meant. I think I cried all the way home. Tears of joy. He hadn't read a single word to me since 2006, and he was reading every sign and billboard on the road. And he slept. He loved to sleep. His sleep was deep, and it was good—something his seizures had robbed him of for so long. I loved to watch him sleep. There was no twitching.

We sat around at home for a few days and just enjoyed our new life with no seizures. He asked to go to the park across the road with his brother, and I could let him without a helmet and without having to worry about a head injury or broken bones. I held on to the helmet because I just wasn't that comfortable with this freedom just yet, but he didn't need it. There were a few seizures here and there, but they seemed like nothing.

He went to school to visit at the end of the week, and he wanted to go back on Monday. My kid, who had hated school since the beginning of time, wanted to go to school. We hadn't expected him to return to school until the next school year, but he wanted to go back. He finished the school year and made more progress in that one month than he had in the last two years.

Once summer rolled around, he was going to the pool every day and was loving every minute of it. He was a bit overly confident and would walk all the way home from the pool by himself when he got tired of swimming. It made me crazy, but it was okay. He was okay. Finally! A little normal.

CHAPTER 25

The Present

* * *

TODAY, AS I LOOK AT my now eighteen-year-old boy, it is bittersweet.

Bitter for so many reasons. Ethan will never live on his own. He will never drive a car, go off to college, or do any of the things every eighteen-year-old looks forward to. He will not write a love letter, send an e-mail, or pick up a girl with his own car. He will not be a dad or a grandpa. He is locked in a five-year-old's mind that continues to have seizures every day. They're not horrible, as they were, but they're bad enough.

We had one glorious seizure-free summer just after his surgery, but the seizures returned. We are so grateful that they are not as bad as they were prior to surgery, but they come almost daily. We deal with it, thankful that they no longer cause injuries. He can feel them coming on, and because they can no longer cross to the other side of the brain, he is usually able to brace himself or hold on to something with his other hand while the other side of his body has a twitchy fit. There are many messes to clean up, but our days are good—far better and less stressful than the early days of helmets and a hundred pills. This boy has been through so much.

It is sweet because he still has that brilliant smile that lights up the room. His eyes still have the same stars that his angels put there all those years ago. Ethan does not know what he is missing as we do. He's not sad about his life. He is *happy*! *Every day is a gift, and that is why we call it the present.* These words are so true!

Ethan is not the same as he was before seizures took over his life, but his bubbly personality, love for life, and the sparkle in his eye still remain. He still talks about his angels and gives them credit for his life, which he enjoys to the fullest every moment, no matter what. Life is good! When he talks of angels, he calls them by name. He knows they are with him. And we choose every day not to hold on to any of the bitterness; we know for sure how blessed we are.

We know that it is only by the grace of God, a magic bone, and a team of angels who worked so hard to save him that we have been allowed the gift of Ethan. He is the heart and soul of our family, and we are blessed.

Mark. He was with the physical therapist and
helped Ethan walk during his hospital stay.

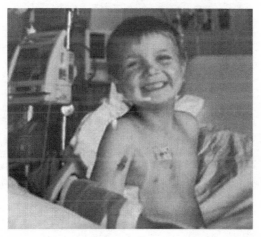

Ethan after surgery to remove his port and the remaining infection

Ethan two weeks into his chemotherapy, sitting in his
favorite green chair. The beginning of hair loss.

The Purple People Eaters.

Sundays in the hospital always required Packers gear.

One of many EEG at home.

Pearl and grandma Agnes

Second Haloween spent in the hospital. Ethan loved to scare the hospital staff with his many costumes and scary props.

Ethan and Snoopy. His "booger" picture is in the background.

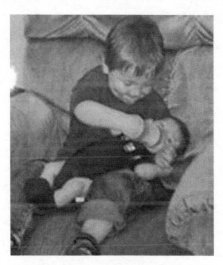

Ethan feeding his baby brother while he
awaits his antifungal treatment.

Ethan protesting another breathing treatment because he's "not even sick anymore".

Ethan just days before his cancer diagnosis.

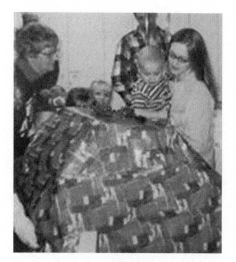

Christmas party.

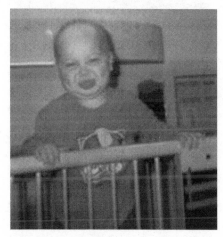

Ethan letting me know he is not taking any pills!

Ethan and his favortie nurse during his hospital stay.

Uncle Skeeter. The "fat guy with the magic bone". His Magic Bone is likely right beneath the birthday cake.

Grandma Elsa

Sharon and Grandma Elsa. Sharon was Ethan's "paramedic" during what was to be his final ambulance ride.

Grandma Elsa and grandma Agnes.

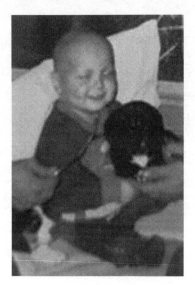

Ethan and Rosie's puppies.

Ethan enjoying his "smashed taters" at his Christmas
party. Sitting with his maternal grandparents.

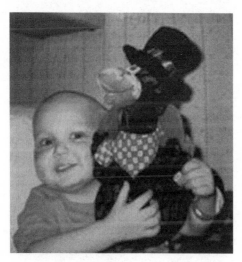

Thanksgiving day in the hospital.

Ethan and his great-grandpa on Thanksgiving.

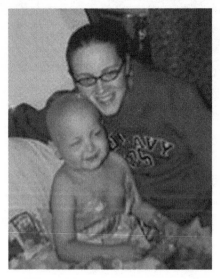

Ethan and Jennifer the day after he was given a terminal diagnosis.

ABOUT THE AUTHOR

*   *   *

JENNIFER BERRETH LIVES WITH HER two sons, Ethan and Aiden, in a small town in eastern North Dakota. Jennifer is currently working and attending college. Ethan is a part-time student and is looking forward to his first job. Aiden is still a student in high school.

Although Jennifer never thought about becoming a writer, she believes that Ethan's story is too important to keep to herself. She hopes it can provide an inspiration and comfort to all who read it.